D0320469

THE
100
VERSE
BIBLE

MARK STIBBE

MONARCH
BOOKS

Oxford, UK & Grand Rapids, Michigan, USA

Copyright © 2010 by Mark Stibbe

The right of Mark Stibbe to be identified as author of this work
has been asserted by him in accordance with the Copyright,
Designs and Patents Act 1988.

All rights reserved. No part of this publication may be
reproduced or transmitted in any form or by any means,
electronic or mechanical, including photocopy, recording or any
information storage and retrieval system, without permission
in writing from the publisher.

First published in the UK in 2010 by Monarch Books
(a publishing imprint of Lion Hudson plc)
Wilkinson House, Jordan Hill Road, Oxford OX2 8DR, England
Tel: +44 (0)1865 302750 Fax: +44 (0)1865 302757
Email: monarch@lionhudson.com
www.lionhudson.com

Reprinted 2010, 2011 (three times).

ISBN 978 1 85424 933 3

Distributed by:
UK: Marston Book Services, PO Box 269, Abingdon, Oxon,
OX14 4YN
USA: Kregel Publications, PO Box 2607, Grand Rapids,
Michigan 49501

Maps on pages 33 and 100 copyright © 1996 Lion Hudson plc/
Tim Dowley Associates

Scripture quotations marked NIV taken from the *Holy Bible,
New International Version*, copyright © 1973, 1978, 1984 by the
International Bible Society. Used by permission of Zondervan
and Hodder & Stoughton Limited. All rights reserved. The
"NIV" and "New International Version" trademarks are
registered in the United States Patent and Trademark Office by
International Bible Society. Use of either trademark requires
the permission of International Bible Society. UK trademark
number 1448790.
Scripture quotations marked KJV taken from the Authorized
Version of the Bible (The King James Bible), the rights in which
are vested in the Crown, are reproduced by permission of the
Crown's Patentee, Cambridge University Press.

The text paper used in this book has been made from wood
independently certified as having come from sustainable
forests.

British Library Cataloguing Data
A catalogue record for this book is available from the British
Library.

Printed and bound in Malta by Gutenberg Press.

Acknowledgments

I want to thank the following for their input. First of all, I am extremely grateful to Catriona Reid, my researcher, for all her wise and insightful comments, and also Vicky Akrill at the Father's House Trust for her comments on the text. Secondly, I want to thank Oliver Griffiths (also at Father's House) for designing some of the diagrams in this book. I also want to thank Tony Collins and the team at Monarch for their support throughout this project. Finally, I'd like to thank my wife Alie and my children for giving me grace to write this little book when I should have been spending time off with them.

About the Father's House Trust

Dr Mark Stibbe is the founder and leader of the Father's House Trust, a charity dedicated to taking the message of the love of the Father all over the world, and to bringing an end to fatherlessness on the earth.

The Father's House Trust seeks to fulfil this vision through five main objectives.

First, the Trust runs schools for leaders that major on the message of the Father's love and the healing of wounded hearts. These are home-based schools in Watford, where the Father's House is located. These schools focus on an encounter with the transformative power of God's love.

Second, the Trust runs schools of the same kind but away from its home base in Watford, and in churches with which it feels a particular partnership. These partner churches are developing all over the world and have a city-changing impact.

Third, the Trust is involved in running annual conferences that serve its vision. These are again based in Watford. In addition, Mark Stibbe and his team contribute to strategic conferences in the UK and abroad.

Fourth, the Trust seeks to engage actively with contemporary culture, and specifically to put fatherhood and fatherlessness on the map in realms such as government, education, the media, the arts, and family life. The Trust seeks to influence the influencers in these realms.

Fifth, the Trust is passionate about ministering to the poor and fighting for the cause of the orphan and widow, in accordance with the biblical mandate to look after those without fathers and those who have lost their husbands (James 1:27).

To know more about the Trust, please consult the website at www.fathershousetrust.com

Introduction:
My Father's Book

In 1947, my adoptive father Philip Stibbe wrote and published his one and only book. He had been schooled well in the art of writing, having studied under C. S. Lewis at Oxford University. In fact, my dad was one of Lewis's star pupils – one of a handful of students who went and had dinner with Lewis on a regular basis. So my father knew how to write elegantly and clearly. Lewis mentored him well.

My father's book is called *Return via Rangoon* and it was first published just after the Second World War. It is the moving account of his time fighting in Major-General Wingate's column behind enemy lines in the often hostile climate and dense jungles of Burma. My father was part of a special force (called the Chindits) tasked to cause as much disruption as possible to the opposing forces. One day there was a battle in a village called Hintha and my father was seriously wounded. A bullet went through his shoulder, just millimetres from his heart, and came out the other side.

My father's prospects were not good. The rule was that if anyone was wounded they had to be left behind in the jungle to fend for themselves. As a special military unit Wingate's column had to move fast and could not be held up by caring for the injured or those debilitated by disease. However, a Gurkha rifleman called Moto volunteered to stay behind with my father to look after him, so he was not left alone.

For days and days Moto looked after my father, foraging through the local villages for food, applying fresh dressings to the wound, fetching water and the like. If Moto had not been there, my father's chances of survival would have been minimal. But this selfless rifleman – about whom we know very little – chose to remain with a wounded officer rather than continue in the greater safety of the marching column. It is hard to express how much my family owes to him.

And it is even harder when I tell you that Moto one day did not come back. My father had seen him go. It seemed like the same routine of finding food and water would happen again, as on previous days. But this time Moto did not return. Worried that something had happened, my father somehow struggled to his feet and walked towards the nearest village. As he approached he saw to his horror that there were two enemy soldiers sitting in the clearing in the centre of the community with their rifles, bayonets fixed. He knew he could not escape so he shouted as loud as he could to alert Moto to the danger.

But Moto could not hear. Later, my father discovered what had happened. Enemy soldiers had been out on patrol because they had been informed that there was a British officer hiding in the jungle. They were eager to capture him so as to interrogate him for information about Wingate's army. But instead of capturing my father they had come upon Moto. They interrogated and tortured him. Moto would not divulge the whereabouts or even the existence of my father. In the end, realizing that there was no way Moto was going to tell them anything, they shot him.

For the next two-and-a-half years my father spent his time in jail as a POW (prisoner of war). His final place of incarceration was the notorious and horrific Rangoon jail. My father was himself questioned and tortured, though he would never talk about it and he wrote only very briefly and generally about it in *Return via Rangoon*. But he suffered badly. Many of his friends and colleagues died of punishment, starvation, and disease. It was unquestionably a dark place.

One day the enemy soldiers took all the prisoners out on a forced march. They told them that they were being moved to a new prisoner-of-war camp. But the reality was that the Allies were advancing on Rangoon jail and the war in the Pacific was nearing its end. As the prisoners walked through the jungle, the enemy soldiers suddenly disappeared. Not long afterwards a column of Allied soldiers approached the emaciated and exhausted prisoners and gave them the news that they had been awaiting for a long time. They were free.

Within several weeks my father was on a plane home, flying over England and then returning to his parents. Within months he was back at Oxford University renewing his English degree studies. During that time he worked on the only book he ever wrote – and what a book it is! After the Bible, *Return via Rangoon* is my most precious book. There is no book other than the Bible that I would rather read.

It may sound odd to mention the Bible and *Return via Rangoon* in the same sentence, but to me they do share some broad similarities. The Bible, to be sure, is very different. It is read by millions of people all over the world. It is one of the best-selling books of all time. In fact, it is really a library of sixty-six books covering the whole of human history, from Paradise Lost in the Garden of Eden (*Genesis*) to Paradise Regained in the Garden of the New Jerusalem (*Revelation*). None of these things can be said of *Return via Rangoon*. The Bible is quite simply unique. It is divinely inspired and infinitely wise.

And yet there are some important similarities. *Return via Rangoon* is my father's book. Even though my father is not with me now physically, I find that in reading its pages I can hear his voice and access his heart. Even more significantly, at the very centre of the story of my father's book is the most self-sacrificial act imaginable – a man who lays down his life for his friend, after being cruelly questioned and abused. *Return via Rangoon* is a wonderful and compelling story told by my father – a story of extraordinary self-sacrificial love and a story of the glorious joy of being set free.

All of these things are true of the Bible too. The Bible, first of all, is the Father's book. Jesus of Nazareth is the subject of the New Testament – the second half of what Christians understand to be the Bible. One of the unique things concerning Jesus is what he revealed to us about the character of God. These words from John's Gospel chapter 14 (verses 1–7) are a telling example:

"Do not let your hearts be troubled. Trust in God; trust also in me. In my Father's house are many rooms; if it were not so, I would have told you. I am going there to prepare a place for you. And if I go and prepare a place for you, I will come back and take you to be with me that you also may be where I am. You know the way to the place where I am going."

Thomas said to him, "Lord, we don't know where you are going, so how can we know the way?"

Jesus answered, "I am the way and the truth and the life. No-one comes to the Father except through me. If you really knew me, you would know my Father as well. From now on, you do know him and have seen him."

These famous Bible verses bring into clear focus the distinctive revelation of God that we find in the teaching of Jesus. They show that the God who designed the universe is the most perfect Father. They show that Jesus is the way to the Father, he is the truth about the Father, and he is the life of the Father. They show that Jesus is also the only way to the Father – a claim that underlines the uniqueness and the singularity of Jesus of Nazareth.

Jesus speaks all the time about this "Father" because "Father" is the premier name for God on his lips. Jesus called God "Father" and taught his disciples to pray "Our Father". The word he would have used is an Aramaic word, *Abba*. *Abba* is the first word uttered by many Middle Eastern children even today. It means "Daddy" and is the most intimate and affectionate form of address.

The Bible is not really a legal book, full of rules and regulations. It is our Father's book. When we read its pages, we hear his voice and we learn more about his character. Even though we cannot see him face to face, we can know him personally because of Jesus. Like Moto, Jesus willingly gave himself up to the most appalling suffering and death, and he did that out of self-sacrificial love so that others could be free. Like *Return via Rangoon*, the Bible is a book written by an adopting father. It is a story of great love and of glorious freedom, for as Jesus said in Luke 4:18–19,

The Spirit of the Lord is on me, because he has anointed me to preach good news to the poor. He has sent me to proclaim freedom for the prisoners and recovery of sight for the blind, to release the oppressed, to proclaim the year of the Lord's favour.

In the pages that follow, I am going to be providing my top 100 Bible verses to change your life – fifty from the Old Testament and fifty from the New. I have chosen verses that I hope will enable you to hear the Father's voice and learn more about his character. I have also chosen verses that point to the big story that the Bible tells and that lead to the key event of the sixty-six books of the Bible – the supreme act of saving love demonstrated by Jesus' death on the Cross.

I want to encourage you to read these verses not

just as ancient wisdom but also as living words from the Father's heart. Read them as words of love to you personally. Let them not only illuminate your head but also warm your heart. Let your Father reach out to you through these Bible verses and allow the Holy Spirit who inspired them to capture your heart with the Love of all loves. Whether they are written in the language of the King James Version (now 400 years old) or in the language of the New International Version (a more contemporary translation), these verses have the capacity to bring love to the unloved and hope to the hopeless. They are part of the love story of Scripture and are personal notes of affection to you.

In the conclusion to this book, I shall take these 100 verses and turn them into an affectionate letter from the Father to you and me. The Bible is not meant to be read legalistically but relationally. My prayer is that you will read the verses in this book and the letter that follows as a personal appeal to you. My prayer is also that you will be brought to the place where you can say yes to the Father's invitation of a relationship with him, and say in the words of 1 John 3:1,

How great is the love the Father has lavished on us, that we should be called children of God! And that is what we are!

THE OLD TESTAMENT

1

In the beginning God created the heaven and the earth.

Genesis 1:1 (KJV)

In the beginning God created the heavens and the earth.

Genesis 1:1 (NIV)

Stories often begin with the phrase, "Once upon a time". The Bible tells the greatest story ever told and its sweep is immense, from the beginning to the end of time. Instead of starting, "Once upon a time", it opens with the memorable words, "In the beginning God created". The word "create" in the Hebrew language here (the language of the Old Testament) is only used of God's creative activity. God fashioned the heavens and the earth from nothing. The universe had a beginning. There is an Alpha Point for the existence of all things. God created all things in order to prepare a home for human beings to inhabit, a place in which he could be our Father and we could be his children. God created the universe and planet earth out of love and for love. Creation out of nothing is a supreme miracle and an extraordinary gift. It marks the start of the love story of the Bible.

2

*And God said, Let us make man in our image,
after our likeness: and let them have dominion over
the fish of the sea, and over the fowl of the air, and
over the cattle, and over all the earth, and over
every creeping thing that creepeth upon the earth.*

Genesis 1:26 (KJV)

**Then God said, "Let us make man in our image,
in our likeness, and let them rule over the fish of
the sea and the birds of the air, over the livestock,
over all the earth, and over all the creatures that
move along the ground."**

Genesis 1:26 (NIV)

After creating the universe, God created human
beings. The Hebrew word for God here is *Elohim*, and
it is plural. That is why it's followed by the statement,
"Let *us* make man in our image." A plural word is
used because God is three persons in one being. He is
triune, "three-in-one" – Father, Son and Holy Spirit –
and he created man. Human beings did not gradually
appear by natural processes. They were created.
Furthermore, while fish, birds, and livestock are said
to be "living creatures" (Genesis 1:20), only human
beings were created "in God's image". This means
that we were created to rule. God is King of creation
and he authorized human beings to rule over the
world in love, to rule in love over all that he has made.
This does not mean a domination and oppression of
creation, but rather a responsible and caring oversight
of the earth. This was our original mission.

15

3

And the LORD God formed man of the dust of the ground, and breathed into his nostrils the breath of life; and man became a living soul.

Genesis 2:7 (KJV)

The LORD God formed the man from the dust of the ground and breathed into his nostrils the breath of life, and the man became a living being.

Genesis 2:7 (NIV)

The climax of God's creative work is the forming of Adam. While everything else in creation is *spoken* into being ("And God said," Genesis 1), the first man is *formed* by God. The word "formed" is the same as that used for a potter forming a pot from clay. God pressed the mud of the ground (*adamah* in Hebrew) and formed Adam (*adam*). And he not only formed Adam, he *filled* him. He breathed into Adam's nostrils. God's life-force entered Adam, making him a living, speaking soul. This shows that the breath that God breathed had spiritual as well as physical power. It wasn't just for human existence on the earth; it was also for intimate communion with God. Thus Adam is a special creation because no other creatures have the spirit of life inbreathed by God personally. Adam was created by God in a unique and intimate way. When Adam came to consciousness, he was face to face with his Father.

4

Now the serpent was more subtil than any beast of the field which the LORD God had made. And he said unto the woman, Yea, hath God said, Ye shall not eat of every tree of the garden?

Genesis 3:1 (KJV)

Now the serpent was more crafty than any of the wild animals the LORD God had made. He said to the woman, "Did God really say, 'You must not eat from any tree in the garden'?"

Genesis 3:1 (NIV)

A demonic interloper arrives in the Garden of Eden, in the visible appearance of a snake. He is identified in the New Testament as "Satan", the "Adversary" (see the Book of Revelation 12:9). Satan is the enemy of God and all things good. He was originally an angel of light called the Morning Star (or "Lucifer", which means Light-bringer). He rebelled against God and fell from heaven, taking one third of the angels with him. Instead of retaliating directly against the Father – a fight he couldn't win – Satan took his revenge by tempting human beings to forsake the special relationship they had with God and to fall into the same orphan state that he had chosen. Tragically, our first human parents fell for the argument, "Did God really say?" From a state of primal innocence and intimacy they chose to sin. Ever since then, all have sinned and been orphaned (separated from the Father) because all are descended from Adam.

5

So he drove out the man; and he placed at the east of the garden of Eden Cherubims, and a flaming sword which turned every way, to keep the way of the tree of life.

Genesis 3:24 (KJV)

After he drove the man out, he placed on the east side of the Garden of Eden cherubim and a flaming sword flashing back and forth to guard the way to the tree of life.

Genesis 3:24 (NIV)

After creation comes catastrophe. Having created a perfect world, the Father is now compelled to banish Adam and Eve from the Garden of Eden. This may seem a somewhat harsh act. How could a loving Father drive his children from the home that he had made for them? The answer lies in the verses leading up to this one. There the Father expresses his concern that Adam and Eve should not be left within reach of another tree in Eden, the Tree of Life. If his children ate of that tree, a tree that brought eternal life, then they would be for ever fallen and for ever unredeemable. So the Father drives Adam and Eve out of the garden and stations *cherubim* – angelic warriors with flashing, fiery swords – to prevent re-entry. From this moment on, man will experience the hardship of toiling for a living and woman the pain of giving birth. These are the consequences of sin and show how serious sin is in the Father's eyes.

6

And the LORD said unto Cain, Where is Abel thy brother? And he said, I know not: Am I my brother's keeper?

Genesis 4:9 (KJV)

Then the LORD said to Cain, "Where is your brother Abel?" "I don't know," he replied. "Am I my brother's keeper?"

Genesis 4:9 (NIV)

Having left Eden, Adam and Eve gave birth to two sons, Cain and then Abel. Abel was more devoted to the LORD than Cain and brought an offering to the LORD that pleased him. Cain's offering, however, did not find favour with God. Cain grew angry and downcast. God warned Cain that sin was crouching at his door and desired to master him. But Cain gave in to sin and killed his brother Abel. It is at this point that God appears and asks Cain where Abel is. Cain responds sarcastically and defensively. But he cannot hide from his Father and he is condemned to be "a restless wanderer on the earth". Here, the very next chapter after the fall of Adam and Eve, we see sin taking hold of humanity. Instead of behaving like a spiritual son, Cain behaves like a spiritual orphan. He is angry, sad, suspicious, jealous, and consigned to a life of striving, loneliness, and fear. Cain is a tragic example of the consequences of the fall. Humans were created to be sons and daughters but are now living like orphans and slaves.

7

I do set my bow in the cloud, and it shall be for a
token of a covenant between me and the earth.

Genesis 9:13 (KJV)

I have set my rainbow in the clouds, and it will
be the sign of the covenant between me and the
earth.

Genesis 9:13 (NIV)

Many generations after Adam and Eve, humanity has
degenerated into extreme darkness. Only Noah is
righteous on the earth. God's Spirit says, "Enough is
enough," and Noah is told to prepare an ark because
God is sending a great flood to destroy the earth.
Noah and his family escape the flood by sailing in
a huge sea-going vessel full of living creatures and
then, after they have landed and started out afresh,
God comes to Noah with a covenant. A covenant is a
promise or contract made by God with human beings.
This is the first of a number of covenants in the Bible.
God designates the rainbow as a perpetual sign of
the covenant to remind us that he will never again
destroy the earth by flooding it. This covenant is for all
people and it foreshadows the future work of Christ.
Just as Noah's family found rescue from the flood by
sheltering in the ark, so all who take refuge in Christ
will be rescued from the consequences of sin.

8

And I will make of thee a great nation, and I will bless thee, and make thy name great; and thou shalt be a blessing.

Genesis 12:2 (KJV)

I will make you into a great nation and I will bless you; I will make your name great, and you will be a blessing.

Genesis 12:2 (NIV)

Abraham is one of the three patriarchs (leading fathers) of Judaism. The patriarchs are Abraham, Isaac, and Jacob. God chooses Abraham and calls him to leave his father's house and go to a country that he will show him. Abraham shows great faith when he obeys this call. Faith is about believing that something is so, even though you cannot yet see it. Abraham believes that there is a country ahead and sets out. It is on the journey that the Father speaks to him and tells him that he is going to make a great nation out of Abraham's offspring. The nation in question is Israel. Through this nation, the Father promises to bless every nation on the earth. After Abraham and Sarah have Isaac, Isaac later has a son called Jacob. Jacob is renamed Israel and has twelve sons who become the fathers of the twelve tribes of Israel. God is a Father who loves to bless and he has chosen Israel to be the nation that brings his blessing to the world.

9

And God said unto Moses, I AM THAT I AM: and he said, Thus shalt thou say unto the children of Israel, I AM hath sent me unto you.

Exodus 3:14 (KJV)

God said to Moses, "I AM WHO I AM. This is what you are to say to the Israelites: ' I AM has sent me to you.'"

Exodus 3:14 (NIV)

Joseph, one of Jacob's twelve sons, is sold into slavery in Egypt, but because he has the gift of interpreting Pharaoh's dreams he is given a prominent position in that country. The rest of Joseph's family eventually joins him in Egypt, and the descendants of Jacob (Israel) live there for the next 400 years. It is at the end of that time that the Israelites become very numerous in Egypt and Pharaoh makes them slaves. God raises Moses – an orphan child – to be the liberator of Israel. Moses' calling comes in Exodus chapter 3 when he hears God speaking to him from a burning bush. God reveals his name, "I Am that I Am" (*Yahweh* in Hebrew, "Jehovah" in English). This name is almost untranslatable and is regarded as utterly sacred. It means something like "For ever" or "Always". Here God tells Moses to go to Pharaoh and to tell him, "The One who is for ever has sent me to you."

10

*And thou shalt say unto Pharaoh, Thus saith the
LORD, Israel is my son, even my firstborn.*

Exodus 4:22 (KJV)

**Then say to Pharaoh, "This is what the LORD says:
Israel is my firstborn son."**

Exodus 4:22 (NIV)

Before Moses leaves the desert of Midian (where he
has encountered the burning bush), God tells him what
to say to Pharaoh. He tells Moses to inform Pharaoh
that Israel is his firstborn son. What is telling about
this statement is that God is clearly saying that he
has a Father–son relationship with his people. He has
adopted Israel as his very own out of all the peoples of
the earth. Through Moses, God tells Pharaoh to let his
son go and uses ten plagues as a warning. Pharaoh
refuses to listen, so his firstborn son and the firstborn
sons of Egypt are killed by the Angel of Death on the
eve of the Exodus (the great escape from Egypt). Just
as Pharaoh had punished God's firstborn son, so now
God punishes Egypt's firstborn. A national crime is
met by a national judgment, because the Father is
jealous for his son. He regards Israel as his son and
wants him to be free from slavery.

11

Now therefore, if ye will obey my voice indeed, and keep my covenant, then ye shall be a peculiar treasure unto me above all people: for all the earth is mine: And ye shall be unto me a kingdom of priests, and an holy nation.

Exodus 19:5–6 (KJV)

"Now if you obey me fully and keep my covenant, then out of all nations you will be my treasured possession. Although the whole earth is mine, you will be for me a kingdom of priests and a holy nation."

Exodus 19:5–6 (NIV)

Three months after the Exodus (the great escape) from Egypt, the Israelites arrive at the Desert of Sinai. The people camp in front of the mountain (Mount Sinai), and Moses goes up to meet with God. God instructs Moses to go back down the mountain and tell the people about the covenant he has made with them. This covenant (the Mosaic covenant) is an agreement between God and his people in which God promises to bless them, provided they obey his commandments. Moses tells the people that if they do that, they will be the Father's treasured possession and a kingdom of priests, a holy nation. The phrase "kingdom of priests" is especially important. The word "priest" here is *cohan* in Hebrew and it literally means "one who draws near to God". The Father longed for a kingdom of people that would draw near to him in love. His heart has always desired intimacy with his people. His heart aches for this to this day.

12

Thou shalt have no other gods before me.

Exodus 20:3 (KJV)

You shall have no other gods before me.

Exodus 20:3 (NIV)

The people of Israel have stopped at Mount Sinai, and Moses once again climbs the mountain to meet with the Father. He is given the Ten Commandments on two tablets of stone. These commandments in summary say this: God's people are to put him first, avoid idolatry, not take his name in vain, keep the sabbath, and honour their parents (commandments 1–5). They are also to refrain from murder, adultery, stealing, slandering their neighbour, and coveting what belongs to someone else (commandments 6–10). The Ten Commandments are designed not to punish God's people but to protect them. These are the boundaries which a loving Father has established for his children. They are also the terms of the covenant with Moses. The first covenant with Noah in Genesis 9 was for everyone. This covenant is for Israel. If the people of Israel obey the covenant, then they will be blessed by their Father in heaven.

Thou shalt have no other gods before me.

Thou shalt not make any graven images.

Thou shalt not take the name of the LORD in vain.

Remember the Sabbath day, to keep it holy.

Honour thy father and mother.

Thou shalt not kill.

Thou shalt not commit adultery.

Thou shalt not steal.

Thou shalt not bear false witness.

Thou shalt not covet.

13

And the LORD passed by before him, and proclaimed, The LORD, The LORD God, merciful and gracious, longsuffering, and abundant in goodness and truth.

Exodus 34:6 (KJV)

And he passed in front of Moses, proclaiming, "The LORD, the LORD, the compassionate and gracious God, slow to anger, abounding in love and faithfulness."

Exodus 34:6 (NIV)

Moses leads God's people as they travel towards the Promised Land. After the people rebel against God and construct a golden calf to worship, God tells Moses he now wants to leave his people. But Moses pleads with God, and God relents, saying that he will still travel with them to the Promised Land. "My Presence will go with you," he says (Exodus 33:14). Moses presses in and prays, "Show me your glory" (Exodus 33:18), and God allows Moses to hide in the cleft of a rock and to see all his goodness pass before his eyes. Here in this magnificent statement from Exodus 34 we see some of the qualities of the Father's glory revealed: mercy, grace, patience, love, and faithfulness. Sometimes it is said that the Old Testament reveals a God of anger, the New, a God of love. This verse shows us that there is grace and love in the Old Testament revelation of God as well.

14

For thou shalt worship no other god: for the LORD, whose name is Jealous, is a jealous God.

Exodus 34:14 (KJV)

Do not worship any other god, for the LORD, whose name is Jealous, is a jealous God.

Exodus 34:14 (NIV)

This verse comes at the end of a passage in Exodus 34 which begins with God saying to Moses, "I am making a covenant with you." God then outlines the nature of the agreement. God's side of the contract is to protect and provide for them in miraculous ways and to drive out the opposing tribes and nations that Israel confronts. Israel's side is to obey everything that God has commanded them. This includes the Ten Commandments in Exodus 20 and all the other laws you can find in Exodus, Leviticus, Numbers, and Deuteronomy (Old Testament books). It especially includes the command not to adopt the idolatrous practices of the pagan nations that Israel meets both on the way to and on arrival in the Promised Land. Israel is to destroy the pagan altars and to worship Yahweh alone, for the Father is jealous for his relationship with Israel, his firstborn son.

15

The LORD make his face shine upon thee, and be gracious unto thee.

Numbers 6:25 (KJV)

The LORD make his face shine upon you and be gracious to you.

Numbers 6:25 (NIV)

This verse records a blessing to be given by Aaron, who was Moses' assistant and the father of a line of priests known as the Aaronic priesthood. This is the oldest blessing in the world and it is also the most beautiful. Here the Father says he will bless and keep (in the sense of "preserve") his people. He will make his face shine upon them like the light of a new day dawning. His thoughts towards them will be thoughts of grace – of love that's rich yet undeserved. He will lift up his face towards his children and he will grant them peace. The word "peace" is the Hebrew word *shalom* and it denotes well-being, wholeness, completeness, and welfare. Its scope includes our relationship with God, with others, with ourselves, and with the world. In the Gospels, Jesus often says, "Peace be to you," which is a common greeting in Hebrew – *shalom aleichem*. Numbers 6:24–26 is truly the greatest of blessings.

16

And in the wilderness, where thou hast seen how that the LORD thy God bare thee, as a man doth bear his son, in all the way that ye went, until ye came into this place.

Deuteronomy 1:31 (KJV)

There you saw how the LORD your God carried you, as a father carries his son, all the way you went until you reached this place.

Deuteronomy 1:31 (NIV)

Deuteronomy is the fifth book of the Old Testament and in Hebrew is called *Devarim*, the Words. The vast majority of it consists of three sermons that Moses preaches as he reviews the previous forty years of wandering in the desert (Deuteronomy 1:1 – 4:43; 4:44 – 28:68; 29:1 – 30:20). The people of Israel are poised to enter the Promised Land, and Moses uses this opportunity to remind them about what God has done for them and what they themselves have done in return. Much of it contains details of the law code that Israel must live by when entering the land. Here, in this memorable verse, Moses reminds the people of God's faithfulness in the past, using the powerful picture of a father carrying his young son on his shoulders. Yahweh is the transcendent and majestic King of the universe. But he is also a caring and involved Father who nurtures, protects, and carries his children.

17

Hear, O Israel: The Lord our God is one Lord.

Deuteronomy 6:4 (KJV)

Hear, O Israel: The Lord our God, the Lord is one.

Deuteronomy 6:4 (NIV)

Another commandment that forms part of the covenant between God and his people is this famous statement known as *Shema Yisrael*, "Hear, O Israel." The declaration twice uses the word *Yahweh*, translated "Lord" in English. Devoted Jews will not speak the name Yahweh out loud and tend to replace it with *Adonai* ("Lord") when speaking or praying, and *YHWH* (the Tetragrammaton, as it is called) in writing. The *Shema* is important because it says that God is one. The word in Hebrew is *echad*, which means either the number one or alone. This highlights the monotheistic nature of Judaism. In other words, it confirms that there is one God, not many gods, and that this God is one being – he is God alone. Interestingly, the word translated "our God" (in the phrase "the Lord our God") is from the Hebrew word *Elohim*, which is a plural word. So even within the *Shema*, Christians believe, God is telling us that he is one and also that he is three in one, as the New Testament will show. He is Father, Son and Holy Spirit.

18

*Be strong and of a good courage; be not afraid,
neither be thou dismayed: for the L*ORD *thy God is
with thee whithersoever thou goest.*

Joshua 1:9 (KJV)

**Be strong and courageous. Do not be terrified; do
not be discouraged, for the L**ORD **your God will be
with you wherever you go.**

Joshua 1:9 (NIV)

After the first five books of the Bible – Genesis, Exodus,
Leviticus, Numbers, and Deuteronomy – comes the
Book of Joshua. At the end of Deuteronomy, Moses
dies before the people have entered the Promised
Land. Moses has laid his hands upon Joshua, and
Joshua had been filled with God's spirit of wisdom.
The people therefore listen to him and he becomes
their leader. In Joshua chapter 1 the LORD tells Joshua
that Moses is now dead and that it is time to enter
and conquer Canaan, the Promised Land. There will
be many battles and trials ahead, but the LORD tells
Joshua to be strong and courageous and not to fear –
words that have been a source of great encouragement
to many believers since. Joshua takes heart and leads
the tribes of Israel into the land. Joshua's name means
"salvation" in Hebrew. The Book of Joshua describes
the invasion and conquest of the land.

MAP OF CANAAN
AND THE TWELVE TRIBES
OF ISRAEL (JOSHUA 14)

G R E A T   S E A

DAN

Tyre

Dan (Laish)

Kedesh

ASHER

NAPHTALI

ZEBULUN

Sea of
Chinnereth

Golan

Shimron

Endor

MANASSEH

Megiddo

ISSACHAR

Ramoth-gilead

M A N A S S E H

Jordan

Shechem

Succoth

Beth-dagon

EPHRAIM

Shiloh

GAD

DAN

Bethel

BENJAMIN

Gibeah

Jericho

Jebus (Jerusalem)

Heshbon

Bezer

J U D A H

Salt Sea

REUBEN

Gaza

Hebron

M O A B

Beersheba

SIMEON

Egypt

E D O M

0   25   50 km

0   10   20   30 miles

—·—·—   Probable boundary of tribe of Israel
⟶   Migration of the tribe of Dan
◉   City of refuge

19

*And the angel of the L*ORD *appeared unto him,
and said unto him, The L*ORD *is with thee, thou
mighty man of valour.*

Judges 6:12 (KJV)

When the angel of the LORD **appeared to Gideon,
he said, "The L**ORD **is with you, mighty warrior."**

Judges 6:12 (NIV)

After Joshua dies, a period of Israel's history
commences in which God's people are oppressed
by other tribes. This era is described in the Book
of Judges. The reason why Israel is so frequently
attacked is because God's people fail to obey the
command to drive out all the other inhabitants of
the Promised Land. Whenever Israel is under the
hammer, God raises up judges – Spirit-empowered
leaders who deliver Israel from oppression. One of the
twelve deliverers is Gideon. When the Israelites are
reduced to hiding in the mountains, the angel of the
LORD comes to Gideon. As Gideon himself confesses,
he is the youngest son of a family that belongs to
the weakest clan in Israel. But the LORD sees him
differently. He sees him as a mighty man of valour.
How often in the Bible the Father uses weak people
to defeat the strong. In his hands, ordinary people
achieve extraordinary things.

THE TWELVE JUDGES OF ISRAEL

Name	Tribe	Oppressed by	Years	Reference
Othniel	Judah	Mesopotamia	8 oppressed, 40 at peace	Judges 3:7-11
Ehud	Benjamin	Moabites	18 oppressed, 80 at peace	Judges 3:12-30
Shamger	Judah	No details		Judges 3:31
Deborah & Barak	Ephraim Naphtali	Canaanites	20 oppressed, 40 at peace	Judges 4:1-5:31
Gideon	Manasseh	Midianites	7 oppressed	Judges 6:1-8:35
Tola	Issachar		23 at peace	Judges 10:1-2
Jair	Gad		22 at peace	40 at peace
Jephthah	Gad	Ammonites	6 at peace	Judges 10:3-5
Ibzan	Judah		7 at peace	Judges 10:6-12:7
Elon	Zebulun		10 at peace	Judges 12:8-10
Abdon	Ephraim		8 at peace	Judges 12:11-12
				Judges 12:13-15
Samson	Dan	Philistines	40 oppressed	Judges 13:1-16:31 20 at peace

20

*And the L*ORD *came, and stood, and called as at other times, Samuel, Samuel. Then Samuel answered, Speak; for thy servant heareth.*

1 Samuel 3:10 (KJV)

The LORD **came and stood there, calling as at the other times, "Samuel! Samuel!" Then Samuel said, "Speak, for your servant is listening."**

1 Samuel 3:10 (NIV)

The period of the judges comes to an end with the birth of Samuel. Eli – who is a priest – is mentoring Samuel at Shiloh, the religious capital of Israel. Samuel is the first of the major biblical prophets and his name means "heard of God". In 1 Samuel chapter 3 we see the boy Samuel being woken up in the night by a voice calling his name. He is probably around thirteen years of age at the time. Three times Samuel gets up and goes to Eli and wakes the priest, thinking that it is him. Eli eventually realizes what is going on and tells Samuel what to say. The fourth time God calls, Samuel tells him he is listening and receives his first prophecy – a judgment against Eli and his rebellious sons. The chapter ends with Eli demanding that Samuel tell him what the LORD has said and Samuel revealing all he has heard from his Heavenly Father.

21

The LORD seeth not as man seeth; for man looketh on the outward appearance, but the LORD looketh on the heart.

1 Samuel 16:7 (KJV)

The LORD does not look at the things man looks at. Man looks at the outward appearance, but the LORD looks at the heart.

1 Samuel 16:7 (NIV)

By now the age of the judges has all but ended. The people of Israel now ask for a king. Samuel is furious because God alone is King. But God tells him to grant their request and Samuel anoints Saul as the first king of Israel. However, Saul's kingship is a failure, so a young boy called David is raised up to succeed Saul. Samuel is called by God to go to the house of Jesse (the father of the future King David), and seven sons of Jesse are brought before him. All of them are able candidates to succeed Saul as king but none of them is the one. Samuel says that the LORD is not impressed by how we look but looks upon our hearts. He is more interested in internal virtue than external prowess. Then the youngest, David, is brought from the hills where he has been looking after the sheep. He is the one, and Samuel anoints him for kingship, whereupon David is filled with the Holy Spirit. Samuel retires to Ramah, where he eventually dies.

22

I will be his father, and he shall be my son: and I will not take my mercy away from him, as I took it from him that was before thee: But I will settle him in mine house and in my kingdom for ever: and his throne shall be established for evermore.

1 Chronicles 17:13–14 (KJV)

I will be his father, and he will be my son. I will never take my love away from him, as I took it away from your predecessor. I will set him over my house and my kingdom for ever; his throne will be established for ever.

1 Chronicles 17:13–14 (NIV)

David does not become king straight after Samuel has anointed him. He has to wait. But when Saul eventually dies, David becomes king. When David has established Jerusalem as the capital city, he begins to long to build a Temple for God's presence there. But Nathan the prophet has a dream and hears the LORD saying that David is not the one to build him a house. His son Solomon is. The LORD promises that he will be Solomon's Father and that Solomon will be his son and that he will always love him. Solomon, the son of David, will have a throne that will be established for ever. This is God's covenant with David. Indeed, one day, Jesus of Nazareth will be born from the line of David and he will be called by many, "Son of David". He will be the King of Kings and his kingdom will be everlasting. He will be the messiah, the anointed one, from the line of the kings of Judah, beginning with David.

OLD TESTAMENT COVENANTS

The Covenant with Noah

Genesis 6:18, 9:9–17
For all the people of the earth
Unconditional (i.e. not dependent on our obedience)
The sign is the rainbow

The Covenant with Abraham

Genesis 12, 15:18–21, 17:1–14
For Abraham and his descendants
Conditional (on Abraham's obedience, and that of his descendants)
The sign is circumcision

The Covenant with Moses

Exodus 19–24
For the nation of Israel (Exodus 19:1–6)
Conditional on the nation's obedience
The sign is the Sabbath

The Covenant with David

2 Samuel 23:5
For David and David's descendants
Conditional (dependent on David and his descendants' obedience)
No sign for this covenant

23

Surely goodness and mercy shall follow me all the days of my life: and I will dwell in the house of the LORD for ever.

Psalm 23:6 (KJV)

Surely goodness and love will follow me all the days of my life, and I will dwell in the house of the LORD for ever.

Psalm 23:6 (NIV)

King David was a great composer of psalms, or what in Hebrew are called the *tehilim*, "praises". Psalm 23 is directly attributed to David, as are most of the first forty-one Psalms. The psalm begins with the well known words, "The LORD is my Shepherd" – a title that David used because of his own early career as a shepherd. David celebrates the LORD's pastoral care in making him lie down in green pastures, leading him beside still waters, restoring his soul, guiding him down right paths, and comforting him in the valley of death. He then praises God for preparing a feast for him and anointing his head with oil, and for filling his cup with overflowing abundance. In the final verse he gives thanks that he is pursued by God's goodness and kindness (*hesed*) and that he will dwell for ever in the Father's house. It is hard to imagine a greater celebration of the Father's role as intimate provider and protector.

24

When my father and my mother forsake me, then the LORD will take me up.

Psalm 27:10 (KJV)

___

Though my father and mother forsake me, the LORD will receive me.

Psalm 27:10 (NIV)

___

Here King David gives praise for the fact that while others may abandon us, our Father in heaven is always there for us and ready to welcome and hold us. David speaks about earthly fathers and mothers here. He acknowledges that they are far from perfect. Some even forsake or desert their children. The word "forsake" is a Hebrew word that David has already used in Psalm 9:9–10: "The LORD is a refuge for the oppressed, a stronghold in times of trouble. Those who know your name will trust in you, for you, LORD, have never *forsaken* those who seek you." In Psalm 27 David follows the same line of thought. First of all he asks the Father not to hide his face from him, not to forsake or reject him. Then he makes the great declaration in verse 10: "Though earthly fathers and mothers may walk out on me, my Heavenly Father will always be there for me." How our fatherless world needs to hear this today!

25

A father of the fatherless, and a judge of the widows, is God in his holy habitation.

Psalm 68:5 (KJV)

A father to the fatherless, a defender of widows, is God in his holy dwelling.

Psalm 68:5 (NIV)

Way back in the time of Moses, God had made it clear that he has a special concern for two groups of people: those who have lost their fathers and those who have lost their husbands (Exodus 22:22). There is something about these two groups of people that evokes special compassion from God. In the Old Testament, orphans are mentioned forty times, widows fifty-six times. The phrase "orphans and widows" occurs thirty times. Here in Psalm 68 King David makes the cause of the orphan and the widow the focus in verse 5. He gives praise that God loves those who have lost their father and those who have lost their husband. He highlights that God is present in love for both groups in his holy dwelling (a word used for the tabernacle, the tent in the wilderness, and the Temple). In our world where there are more fatherless people than ever, there is a pressing need to rediscover this expression of the Father's merciful heart.

26

Like as a father pitieth his children, so the LORD pitieth them that fear him.

Psalm 103:13 (KJV)

As a father has compassion on his children, so the LORD has compassion on those who fear him.

Psalm 103:13 (NIV)

Psalm 103 is one of the most famous of David's psalms. It is full of memorable lines: "The LORD is compassionate and gracious, slow to anger, abounding in love" (verse 8). "As far as the east is from the west, so far has he removed our transgressions from us" (verse 12). But one of the most powerful verses of all is the one here, which underlines God's fatherly care for those who "fear him". The word "fear" is widely misunderstood. The verb is used three times in this psalm and it really denotes absolute reverence. God is a mighty, sovereign, royal Father – the greatest Father in the universe. As such, he is to be respected. At the same time, not only is he worthy of our holy reverence, he is also longing for our love and affection. God is a Father who evokes holy fear. But he is also a Father who has loving compassion on his children. David truly knew the heart of God!

27

I will praise thee; for I am fearfully and wonderfully made: marvellous are thy works; and that my soul knoweth right well.

Psalm 139:14 (KJV)

I praise you because I am fearfully and wonderfully made; your works are wonderful, I know that full well.

Psalm 139:14 (NIV)

Psalm 139 is perhaps the most intimate of the psalms that David composed. The overriding theme of the poem is David's praise for God's personal interest in every aspect of his life. From his mother's womb onwards, God has been watching over King David's life. Here God's omniscient (all-knowing, verses 1–6), omnipresent (verses 7–12), omnipotent (all-powerful, verses 13–15) nature is exalted in the most sublime poetic language. David was writing in the context of wicked accusers (verses 19–22). This psalm of praise is his response. He knows that whatever people may say about God, and whatever they may say about us, God knows us, watches over us, guards and guides us like a perfect Father. In verses 13–16 God is depicted as a weaver who carefully creates the intricate tapestry of our lives. We are indeed fearfully and wonderfully made by the hands of the world's greatest Father. From the womb to the tomb, our Father invests in our lives personally.

28

Give me now wisdom and knowledge, that I may go out and come in before this people: for who can judge this thy people, that is so great?

2 Chronicles 1:10 (KJV)

Give me wisdom and knowledge, that I may lead this people, for who is able to govern this great people of yours?

2 Chronicles 1:10 (NIV)

After King David's death, Solomon succeeds his father as king of Israel. He goes to Gibeon, where the bronze altar that Bezalel had made in Moses' day is located, and offers a thousand burned offerings to the LORD. That night, the LORD appears to him in a dream and tells him to ask for whatever he wants. This is the dream of all dreams. Solomon can have anything in the whole world. What would you have asked for? King Solomon asks for wisdom and knowledge to lead God's people. What a great request! All leaders, in whatever sphere, should ask for these two essential leadership qualities. And God grants Solomon his prayer, because he has not asked for money and fame, for victory over his enemies, or for a long life. He has asked for something worthy of a great leader. From Gibeon, Solomon returns to Jerusalem to reign in Israel. Shortly afterwards he starts to construct the Temple in Jerusalem.

29

Trust in the LORD with all thine heart; and lean not unto thine own understanding.

Proverbs 3:5 (KJV)

Trust in the LORD with all your heart and lean not on your own understanding.

Proverbs 3:5 (NIV)

The Book of Proverbs comes from a section of the Old Testament known as the Writings. The original title in the Hebrew Bible is "The Proverbs of Solomon". Proverbs chapter 3 begins with Solomon saying to the one he is mentoring, "My son, do not forget my teaching, but keep my commands in your heart, for they will prolong your life many years and bring you prosperity" (verses 1–2). Here Solomon urges his son to hold fast to the *torah*, a word which means divine instruction and direction and is often translated "Law". The son is to maintain a life of spiritual devotion by writing this teaching on his heart. He is also to put his trust in the LORD. The word means literally that he is to throw himself upon the LORD. He is not to rely on his own intellectual understanding but build his life on the Father's *hokmah*, or wisdom. In the New Testament, Jesus Christ is presented as Wisdom in person (1 Corinthians 1:24).

30

Many waters cannot quench love, neither can the floods drown it: if a man would give all the substance of his house for love, it would utterly be contemned.

Song of Songs 8:7 (KJV)

Many waters cannot quench love; rivers cannot wash it away. If one were to give all the wealth of his house for love, it would be utterly scorned.

Song of Songs 8:7 (NIV)

The Song of Songs is a book also known as the Song of Solomon. There are two main characters in the poem: the woman and the man who loves her. There is also a dramatic chorus, "the daughters of Jerusalem". The Song of Songs is accordingly a collection of Hebrew love poems attributed to King Solomon. It portrays the journey from courtship to consummation. The poem as a whole has often been regarded as an allegory of God's relationship with Israel and Christ's relationship with his bride, the church. It is a very short book (only 117 verses in length). Here the poet sings of the great power of true love. The many waters of trials and tests cannot put out the flame of love, earthly or divine. No material wealth can compare with it. Love is as strong as death. No wonder Martin Luther called the Song of Songs *das Hohelied*, the High Song.

31

If my people, which are called by my name, shall humble themselves, and pray, and seek my face, and turn from their wicked ways; then will I hear from heaven, and will forgive their sin, and will heal their land.

2 Chronicles 7:14 (KJV)

If my people, who are called by my name, will humble themselves and pray and seek my face and turn from their wicked ways, then will I hear from heaven and will forgive their sin and will heal their land.

2 Chronicles 7:14 (NIV)

Solomon calls the people of Israel to start work on the Temple in Jerusalem, and from 2 Chronicles chapter 2 to chapter 4 the Temple is built. In the two chapters prior to 2 Chronicles 7:14, Solomon dedicates the Temple that the people have built. At the end of 2 Chronicles 6, Solomon prays that the Lord will come and make his resting place in this magnificent architectural wonder. In 2 Chronicles 7, the cloud of the glory of God fills the Temple and all the priests are overwhelmed. All are singing, "His love endures for ever." Not long after, God appears to Solomon in a dream and tells him what to do whenever his blessing lifts from Israel. He says the people must humble themselves, pray, seek his face, and turn from wickedness. If they do that, his blessing will be restored. Their sins will be forgiven and the land will be healed. This verse has been the inspiration for millions who long for the Father to come and visit his people in power.

32

*And the L*ORD *was angry with Solomon, because his heart was turned from the L*ORD *God of Israel, which had appeared unto him twice.*

1 Kings 11:9 (KJV)

The LORD **became angry with Solomon because his heart had turned away from the L**ORD**, the God of Israel, who had appeared to him twice.**

1 Kings 11:9 (NIV)

This is a critical verse in the unfolding drama of the Old Testament. Solomon has disobeyed God. He has multiplied horses, wives, and gold – the very things that God commanded the kings not to do in Deuteronomy 17:16–17. Solomon has fallen for the three main idols of power, sex, and money. He should not have pursued these toxic attachments, especially since God had appeared twice to him – once before he had dedicated the Temple (1 Kings 3:5) and once after (1 Kings 9:2). But Solomon sins, and the divine punishment for this is that there will be a tearing of his kingdom. This is exactly what happens. When Solomon dies and his son Rehoboam succeeds him, the kingdom is torn in two. The southern part (called Judah) remains centred on Jerusalem. The northern part (called Israel) is formed when ten of the twelve tribes refuse to submit to the rule of the king of Judah.

MAP OF THE DIVISION OF THE TWO KINGDOMS

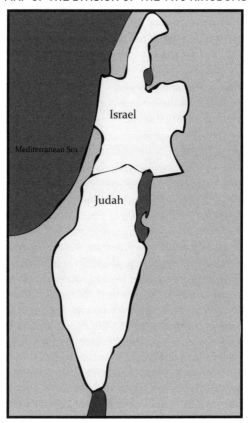

33

And he said, I have been very jealous for the LORD God of hosts: because the children of Israel have forsaken thy covenant, thrown down thine altars, and slain thy prophets with the sword; and I, even I only, am left; and they seek my life, to take it away.

1 Kings 19:14 (KJV)

He replied, "I have been very zealous for the LORD God Almighty. The Israelites have rejected your covenant, broken down your altars, and put your prophets to death with the sword. I am the only one left, and now they are trying to kill me too."

1 Kings 19:14 (NIV)

From the year 922 BC to 722 BC the northern kingdom is ruled by nineteen kings. During the reign of one of these, called Ahab (869–850 BC), Elijah the prophet is raised up by God. Elijah's name means "My God is Yahweh". Ahab was a sinful king who had married Jezebel, a priestess of the pagan god Baal. Ahab allowed his wife to create a large entourage of pagan priests and prophets devoted to Baal – a god associated with sexual immorality. It is into this dire situation that Elijah is called to pronounce the Father's warnings and judgments. 1 Kings 19:14 comes shortly after Elijah's successful challenge to the 450 prophets of Baal on Mount Carmel. Elijah is on the run from the wicked queen Jezebel and hiding in a cave for the night. There he tells the LORD how he has been standing alone against the tide of darkness in the nation because he is jealous for the LORD's name.

34

Now there cried a certain woman of the wives of the sons of the prophets unto Elisha, saying, Thy servant my husband is dead; and thou knowest that thy servant did fear the LORD: and the creditor is come to take unto him my two sons to be bondmen.

2 Kings 4:1 (KJV)

The wife of a man from the company of the prophets cried out to Elisha, "Your servant my husband is dead, and you know that he revered the LORD. But now his creditor is coming to take my two boys as his slaves."

2 Kings 4:1 (NIV)

Elisha was Elijah's successor. His name means "My God is Salvation". Elijah is taken up to heaven in a chariot of fire (2 Kings 2:11–12). Having grieved his mentor's departure, Elisha takes hold of the prophetic mantle given to him by Elijah and begins his ministry in the northern kingdom. For sixty years he holds the office of prophet in Israel (892–832 BC). Elisha is given a double blessing by Elijah, so we find twice the number of miracles in Elisha's ministry as in his predecessor's. In 2 Kings 4 Elisha performs a miracle of provision for a widow. Her two sons have become orphans. They are now fatherless and they are also in danger of being sold into slavery. Elisha supernaturally supplies a superabundance of oil for the widow and her sons, so she can pay her debts and live on what remains. Elisha's conduct reveals how closely he embodies the Father's compassion for the widow and the orphan.

35

*When Israel was a child, then I loved him, and
called my son out of Egypt.*

Hosea 11:1 (KJV)

**When Israel was a child, I loved him, and out of
Egypt I called my son.**

Hosea 11:1 (NIV)

The northern kingdom falls to the Assyrian Army
in 722 BC. Samaria, its capital city, is destroyed. In
the sixty years before Israel's fall, three prophets
emerge in Israel to prophesy to the people about the
impending destruction that their sins have brought
upon themselves. Their names are Jonah, Amos
and Hosea. These three men form part of the "minor
prophets" in the Old Testament. Hosea's name means
"Salvation is of the Lord". He married an unfaithful
prostitute called Gomer in order to highlight the
unfaithfulness of Israel to her God. The Book of Hosea
is a harsh warning to Israel to stop following after
foreign gods and to remain faithful to Yahweh. In this
poignant verse God speaks as a father, reminding his
people that he adopted Israel as his son and led him
out of slavery. But now Israel is deciding to forsake
his sonship and choose slavery instead. This will have
terminal consequences for the northern kingdom.

MINOR PROPHETS

Group	Book	Approximate dates
Prophets of Israel before the Assyrians conquered Israel	Jonah (preached to Nineveh)	780–850 BC
	Amos	765–750 BC
	Hosea	755–715 BC
Prophets of Judah before the Babylonians conquered Judah	Obadiah	840 BC
	Joel	835–796 BC
	Micah	740–690 BC
	Nahum	630–612 BC
	Habakkuk	606–604 BC
	Zephaniah	625 BC
Prophets in Judah after the return of the Jews from Exile in Babylon	Haggai	520 BC
	Zechariah	515 BC
	Malachi	430 BC

36

Therefore the Lord himself shall give you a sign;
Behold, a virgin shall conceive, and bear a son,
and shall call his name Immanuel.

Isaiah 7:14 (KJV)

Therefore the Lord himself will give you a sign:
The virgin will be with child and will give birth to a
son, and will call him Immanuel.

Isaiah 7:14 (NIV)

While the northern kingdom falls to the Assyrians in
722 BC, the southern kingdom of Judah continues until
586 BC, when it falls to the Babylonians. A number of
prophets are called by God to speak to the people of
Judah over the centuries between 722 and 586 BC.
One of the greatest of these prophets is Isaiah, who
prophesied six centuries before Christ. His message
is one of warning as well as hope. Isaiah 7:14 has long
been regarded by Christians as one such prophecy of
hope. Here Isaiah prophesies to the house of David,
saying that a virgin will conceive and have a son whose
name will be "Immanuel", which means "God with
us". The word "virgin" is *almah* in Hebrew, meaning
"a young unmarried woman". Since in the culture of
the time such a woman would certainly be a virgin,
the KJV and NIV are right to translate it "virgin". Many
centuries later this prophecy will be applied to the
Virgin Mary, mother of Jesus (Matthew 1:23).

37

For unto us a child is born, unto us a son is given: and the government shall be upon his shoulder: and his name shall be called Wonderful, Counsellor, The mighty God, The everlasting Father, The Prince of Peace.

Isaiah 9:6 (KJV)

For to us a child is born, to us a son is given, and the government will be on his shoulders. And he will be called Wonderful Counsellor, Mighty God, Everlasting Father, Prince of Peace.

Isaiah 9:6 (NIV)

About 600 years before Jesus was born, Isaiah the prophet declared that a male child would be born. This son would reign on King David's throne and his rule would be everlasting. King David's reign lasted from about 1050 to 1010 BC, and during that time the LORD had made a covenant with David that his throne would be everlasting. Christians believe that this prophecy is ultimately fulfilled in Jesus of Nazareth. Jesus reigns for ever. His kingdom (the kingdom of God) is eternal. Moreover, Jesus deserves all the names that Isaiah attributes to this unique, future, royal son: Wonderful, Counsellor, Mighty God, Everlasting Father, Prince of Peace. Notice "Everlasting Father". Jesus said, "Anyone who has seen me has seen the Father" (John 14:9). Jesus would come as the Son of the Everlasting Father who reveals what the Father is truly like. Jesus would come as both messiah and LORD – as God in human flesh.

38

But he was wounded for our transgressions, he was bruised for our iniquities: the chastisement of our peace was upon him; and with his stripes we are healed.

Isaiah 53:5 (KJV)

But he was pierced for our transgressions, he was crushed for our iniquities; the punishment that brought us peace was upon him, and by his wounds we are healed.

Isaiah 53:5 (NIV)

For Christians, the most important of all Isaiah's prophecies is in Isaiah 53. Here Isaiah has a vision of a Suffering Servant of Yahweh. He sees that this man will grow up like any ordinary, unremarkable mortal, that he will be despised and rejected and become a man familiar with human suffering. He will be considered afflicted by God as he carries our sorrows and is wounded for our transgressions. But it will also be seen that the penalty he bore in our place would give us peace, and the pain that he suffered would bring us healing. Christians believe that all this points to the birth, life, and death of Jesus of Nazareth. On the Cross, Jesus took our punishment, he made the supreme sacrifice, so that we might be reconciled to our Father in heaven. Jesus suffered terribly to redeem us all from our sins. The whole of the Old Testament leads towards this great truth.

39

But now, O LORD, thou art our father; we are the clay, and thou our potter; and we all are the work of thy hand.

Isaiah 64:8 (KJV)

Yet, O LORD, you are our Father. We are the clay, you are the potter; we are all the work of your hand.

Isaiah 64:8 (NIV)

Sometimes it is said that the revelation of God as Father comes only in the New Testament. This is an exaggeration. In Isaiah 64 the prophet reflects on how the people of the southern kingdom have departed from God's ways. He reflects on how God in the past has acted on their behalf, but now Judah is far from God because of the unrighteousness of the people. Yet God is the one who forms and fathers his people. He formed his people as a potter forms a lump of clay. He fathers his people as a loving Father should. So even while Judah's cities are laid waste and the Temple is in ruins, Isaiah can say, "But you are our Father, though Abraham does not know us or Israel acknowledge us; you, O LORD, are our Father, our Redeemer from of old is your name" (Isaiah 63:16). Isaiah exalts God as loving Father.

40

But thou, Bethlehem Ephratah, though thou be little among the thousands of Judah, yet out of thee shall he come forth unto me that is to be ruler in Israel; whose goings forth have been from of old, from everlasting.

Micah 5:2 (KJV)

But you, Bethlehem Ephrathah, though you are small among the clans of Judah, out of you will come for me one who will be ruler over Israel, whose origins are from of old, from ancient times.

Micah 5:2 (NIV)

Micah prophesies in Judah during the reign of King Hezekiah (see Jeremiah 26:18). Micah lived at a time of instability in his region. The Assyrian army had conquered the northern kingdom, and the rich were exploiting the poor in the southern kingdom, where Micah lived. Micah was appalled by the people's disobedience to God's covenant and spoke out against the injustices of his day. In Micah 5:2 he prophesies that a ruler in Israel will come from the tiny town of Bethlehem (meaning "house of bread") Ephrathah (meaning "fertile"). Micah narrows the birthplace of the messiah to the town where David was born and crowned. In Matthew 2:1–6 we see this prophecy fulfilled in the birth of Jesus. The Jewish Talmud (a record of the teaching of the Rabbis, second century BC) also spoke of this: "The King Messiah... from where does he come forth? From the royal city of Bethlehem in Judah." Micah prophesies the birthplace of Jesus the messiah.

41

The LORD thy God in the midst of thee is mighty;
he will save, he will rejoice over thee with joy;
he will rest in his love, he will joy over thee with
singing.

Zephaniah 3:17 (KJV)

The LORD your God is with you, he is mighty to
save. He will take great delight in you, he will
quiet you with his love, he will rejoice over you
with singing.

Zephaniah 3:17 (NIV)

Zephaniah is a "minor prophet" who prophesied in the southern kingdom during the reign of Josiah in the seventh century BC. His name means "He whom the Lord has hidden". The two kings prior to Josiah had brought idolatry into Judah and Jerusalem, especially the worship of Baal. Zephaniah's book is only three chapters long but the overriding theme is one of impending judgment – judgment for Judah and Jerusalem for their sins (chapter 1), judgment for the nations of the world (chapter 2). In chapter 3 (verses 1–8) Zephaniah rounds on the ruling classes and the priests in Jerusalem, giving them dire warnings, before turning to the long-term future and the coming of the kingdom of God in the future (verses 9–20). On the day of the coming of God's kingdom, God's presence will be felt and his delight over Jerusalem will be known. He will refresh his people with his love and will spin around and sing for joy over them, like a deliriously happy Father.

42

*For I know the thoughts that I think toward you,
saith the LORD, thoughts of peace, and not of evil,
to give you an expected end.*

Jeremiah 29:11 (KJV)

---

*"For I know the plans I have for you," declares the
LORD, "plans to prosper you and not to harm you,
plans to give you hope and a future."*

Jeremiah 29:11 (NIV)

Jeremiah is known as one of the "major prophets".
He was called by God to confront the people of Judah
concerning their worship of idols (625–575 BC). In this
and in many other ways they had broken the covenant.
God therefore declares that they are going to
experience destruction. The disaster of the Babylonian
siege of Jerusalem still lay ahead of them, and the
people didn't take kindly to his words. Jeremiah was
attacked and imprisoned by his own people, but when
King Nebuchadnezzar sacked Jerusalem he released
Jeremiah from prison and treated him well. In spite
of the fact that Jeremiah is known as "the weeping
prophet", his prophecy in 29:11 is full of hope. He
declares that after seventy years, Babylon's days will
be completed and the Jewish remnant will return
from exile to the land. God knows the plans he has
for his people and they are for a hope and a future.
Whenever believers face hardship, there is always
something for them to hope for.

43

But this shall be the covenant that I will make with the house of Israel; After those days, saith the LORD, I will put my law in their inward parts, and write it in their hearts; and will be their God, and they shall be my people.

Jeremiah 31:33 (KJV)

"This is the covenant that I will make with the house of Israel after that time," declares the LORD. "I will put my law in their minds and write it on their hearts. I will be their God, and they will be my people."

Jeremiah 31:33 (NIV)

Jeremiah prophesies that there are days coming when the LORD will bring Judah and Israel back from exile to the land of their forefathers. God promises to restore the fortunes of the land to what they were before the exile. God promises that a righteous branch will sprout from David's line – a promise of the birth of Jesus the messiah. He declares that he has loved his people with an everlasting love. The Temple will be restored and people will make pilgrimage there with shouts of joy, and all because Israel is the Father's dear son (Jeremiah 31:20). In those days Jeremiah prophesies that the LORD will form a new covenant with his people. This time the law will no longer be something external, such as writing on stone. It will be an internal reality as the Spirit of God writes it on their hearts. Six hundred years later this was to be fulfilled when the Spirit of God was poured out on the Day of Pentecost, and it is still being fulfilled today!

THE 100 VERSE BIBLE

44

Now it came to pass in the thirtieth year, in the fourth month, in the fifth day of the month, as I was among the captives by the river of Chebar, that the heavens were opened, and I saw visions of God.

Ezekiel 1:1 (KJV)

In the thirtieth year, in the fourth month on the fifth day, while I was among the exiles by the Kebar River, the heavens were opened and I saw visions of God.

Ezekiel 1:1 (NIV)

Eventually the southern kingdom follows the same path to destruction as that taken by Israel. As the sixth century BC begins, Babylon is the world's superpower. Led by Nebuchadnezzar, the Babylonian army sacks Jerusalem, destroys the Temple, and takes the priceless treasures of the Temple, including the Ark of the Covenant, back to Babylon. The remnant in Judah is taken as captives into exile in 586 BC. Babylon rules the Promised Land until 539 BC. In the sixty years or so from 600 to 539 BC, prophets such as Ezekiel are raised up by God to speak to the Jewish people. Ezekiel's name means "God will strengthen", a fitting one for his message. Ezekiel received many fortifying visions while he was in Babylon – such as the dry bones coming to life (Ezekiel 37) and the restored Temple as the source of a life-giving river (Ezekiel 47). Here in the first verse of his book, Ezekiel describes how in Babylon the heavens were opened and he had visions of God.

45

A new heart also will I give you, and a new spirit will I put within you: and I will take away the stony heart out of your flesh, and I will give you an heart of flesh.

Ezekiel 36:26 (KJV)

I will give you a new heart and put a new spirit in you; I will remove from you your heart of stone and give you a heart of flesh.

Ezekiel 36:26 (NIV)

One of Ezekiel's most important prophecies of hope concerns a future time when God will put a new spirit within the hearts of his people. Many of the people of Judah were now in exile in Babylon (modern Iraq). This was because they had engaged in idolatrous practices and had broken God's covenant. But Ezekiel brings good news. There's a day coming when the LORD will restore the land to them, and Israel and Judah will be reunited into one nation back home, under the leadership of one king. There will be a spiritual renewal in which God will sprinkle clean water on them, and he will give them a new heart and a new spirit (Ezekiel 36:24–29). In verse 27 he says that he will put his Spirit in people's hearts so that they will *want* to obey his laws. The gift of the indwelling Spirit will be given as Jesus establishes the new covenant through his death on the Cross.

46

The king answered unto Daniel, and said, Of a truth it is, that your God is a God of gods, and a Lord of kings, and a revealer of secrets, seeing thou couldest reveal this secret.

Daniel 2:47 (KJV)

The king said to Daniel, "Surely your God is the God of gods and the Lord of kings and a revealer of mysteries, for you were able to reveal this mystery."

Daniel 2:47 (NIV)

Daniel is in captivity in Babylon along with the survivors ("the remnant") of the people of Judah. Daniel chapter 2 describes a test given to Daniel. King Nebuchadnezzar has a dream which troubles him. He calls his court astrologers to interpret it for him. However, he does not tell them the dream. They fail in the task, so Daniel prays. God tells him the dream and its interpretation. The dream is of the destruction of a statue with a head of gold, chest and arms of silver, belly and thighs of bronze, feet of iron and clay. Daniel tells the king that this refers to his kingdom (the gold head) and four others that will follow, all of which will come to an end. But there will be a kingdom that will last for ever (the kingdom of God). Daniel passes his test (and all the others described in this book) and the pagan king declares that Daniel's God is the God of gods, the Lord of Kings, and the Revealer of Mysteries.

47

Then he answered and spake unto me, saying, This is the word of the LORD unto Zerubbabel, saying, Not by might, nor by power, but by my spirit, saith the LORD of hosts.

Zechariah 4:6 (KJV)

So he said to me, "This is the word of the LORD to Zerubbabel: 'Not by might nor by power, but by my Spirit,' says the LORD Almighty."

Zechariah 4:6 (NIV)

In 538 BC, the Babylonians had been replaced by the Persians as the world's superpower. This brought the Persian King Cyrus to power. He released the Jewish remnant from their captivity in exile. Led by Zerubbabel and Joshua, 50,000 Jews returned from Babylon to the land and for two years worked on rebuilding the Temple. Then in 536 BC the work ground to a halt. For over fifteen years the two leaders were discouraged at the inactivity of God's people, until two prophets – Zechariah and Haggai – came and spoke words of encouragement. Here Zechariah tells Zerubbabel that the new Temple will be built but that this will be achieved not by human power but by the Spirit of God. Thereafter God's Spirit stirred the people to work and the Second Temple was completed in 516 BC. All this highlights the believer's absolute dependence on the Holy Spirit in building anything for the Lord of Hosts (literally, "the Lord of the Armies of Heaven").

48

Then he said unto them, Go your way, eat the fat, and drink the sweet, and send portions unto them for whom nothing is prepared: for this day is holy unto our Lord: neither be ye sorry; for the joy of the LORD is your strength.

Nehemiah 8:10 (KJV)

Nehemiah said, "Go and enjoy choice food and sweet drinks, and send some to those who have nothing prepared. This day is sacred to our Lord. Do not grieve, for the joy of the LORD is your strength."

Nehemiah 8:10 (NIV)

After Zerubbabel and Joshua had completed the rebuilding of the Temple in 516 BC, it was time for the city of Jerusalem to be restored as well. In 459 BC Ezra, a Jewish priest still in Babylon, led about 10,000 of his expatriates back to the land. He brought the Jewish people back to the law and challenged them to be a holy nation at a time when there were intermarriages taking place with other nations. Ezra reappears in Nehemiah chapter 8 when the city walls have been rebuilt by Nehemiah. The Book of the Law is brought out, and Ezra and the Levites read it night and day and explain its meaning to the people. All the people begin to weep because they are so powerfully moved by the words of God's Book. But Nehemiah (the governor) and Ezra (the priest) tell them to stop weeping and to start rejoicing. The joy of the Lord is their strength. It is a hallmark of God's people. So now it's time to celebrate!

49

And it shall come to pass afterward, that I will pour out my spirit upon all flesh; and your sons and your daughters shall prophesy, your old men shall dream dreams, your young men shall see visions.

Joel 2:28 (KJV)

And afterwards, I will pour out my Spirit on all people. Your sons and daughters will prophesy, your old men will dream dreams, your young men will see visions.

Joel 2:28 (NIV)

Joel's name means "Yahweh is God". Very little is known about who he was or when he prophesied. Some argue that he prophesied in the eighth century BC. Others propose that he prophesied after the exile, in the fifth century BC. Joel 2:28 is perhaps the most famous of his prophecies. Like other Old Testament prophets, Joel prophesies a day when God will pour out his Spirit (see also Isaiah 32:15; 44:1–5, and Ezekiel 39:29). Joel 2:28 forms part of a promise that Yahweh will bless his people with his visible, glorious presence and never again allow them to be put to shame. The fulfilment of this will be in Jerusalem hundreds of years later, when the Holy Spirit falls upon the 120 disciples of Jesus on the Day of Pentecost (see Acts 2:1–21). Then the long drought of the Holy Spirit, lasting 400 years, will come to an end with a deluge of the Father's love from heaven.

50

And he shall turn the heart of the fathers to the children, and the heart of the children to their fathers, lest I come and smite the earth with a curse.

Malachi 4:6 (KJV)

He will turn the hearts of the fathers to their children, and the hearts of the children to their fathers; or else I will come and strike the land with a curse.

Malachi 4:6 (NIV)

With these words of the fifth-century prophet Malachi, the Old Testament closes. It opened with the creation of the world and the fall of humankind. The Adversary of God tempted Eve and Adam and they fell from their position of daughter and son into the orphan state. Thereafter the Father adopted a people as his cherished firstborn son. From Abraham onwards, the people of Israel have been the focus of the Father's covenant love. In spite of that, Israel falls time and time again for the Adversary's temptations. Throughout the Old Testament the Adversary works behind the scenes to pull God's people again and again into the orphan state. But the Old Testament ends with a great prospect – a time when there will be reconciliation between children and their earthly fathers, and – by implication – between human beings and the Perfect Father. It will be with the coming of Jesus – God's One and Only Son – that this promise is fulfilled.

THE NEW TESTAMENT

NEW TESTAMENT TIME LINE

40	BC	Herod the Great made King of Judea by Marc Antony
27	BC	Founding of the Roman Empire
20	BC	Herod the Great starts Temple rebuilding programme
6	BC	Jesus' birth
4	BC	King Herod the Great dies
26-36	AD	Pontius Pilate is governor of Judea
26-28	AD	John the Baptist's ministry
27-30	AD	Jesus' ministry
30	AD	Crucifixion and resurrection of Jesus
31	AD	Stephen martyred (Acts 6-8)
34-35	AD	Conversion of Saul (who becomes Paul, Acts 9)
38	AD	Peter baptizes the first Gentiles (Acts 10)
44-46	AD	Paul's first Missionary Journey
47	AD	First recorded use of the word "Christian" in Antioch
48-49	AD	Council at Jerusalem (Acts 15)
49-52	AD	Paul's second Missionary Journey
53-57	AD	Paul's third Missionary Journey
58-68	AD	Paul's final Missionary Journey and Martyrdom in Rome
70	AD	Destruction of the Temple in Jerusalem

51

For unto you is born this day in the city of David a Saviour, which is Christ the Lord.

Luke 2:11 (KJV)

Today in the town of David a Saviour has been born to you; he is Christ the Lord.

Luke 2:11 (NIV)

There are few historical events more important than the birth of Jesus in Bethlehem. Micah the prophet had declared that this town would be the birthplace of a ruler in Israel. This was regarded by the earliest Christians as a messianic prophecy (a prediction concerning the coming messiah). Here Luke describes a group of shepherds out on the hills who have an encounter with angels. This is a surprise in itself because the shepherd's profession was a poor and despised one on earth. Not so in heaven. The angels tell the shepherds that the one who has just been born in Bethlehem is none other than the LORD. In the world of the shepherds, only one man was called "Lord" by the people of the day: the Roman emperor, and he ruled through force. But there is one born in Bethlehem who is greater than Caesar, and who will rule the world with the power of love, not the love of power.

52

And the Word was made flesh, and dwelt among us, (and we beheld his glory, the glory as of the only begotten of the Father,) full of grace and truth.

John 1:14 (KJV)

The Word became flesh and made his dwelling among us. We have seen his glory, the glory of the One and Only, who came from the Father, full of grace and truth.

John 1:14 (NIV)

At the beginning of history, God spoke the world into being. Through the power of his word, everything was created from nothing. At the beginning of John's Gospel, Jesus is called "the Word" (*Logos* in Greek, the language of the New Testament). Jesus is the Word that was with the Father at the beginning of time. Jesus is the Word who is God from eternity to eternity. The one born as a baby in Bethlehem is therefore no ordinary mortal. He is not just the greatest of all prophets and teachers. He is the divine *Logos* made flesh. He is God with skin on. He is the infinite become an infant. In Jesus, Yahweh has come to camp out among us. John (the writer of the Gospel) and those with him lived with Jesus-the-Word and saw God's glory in his human flesh. Jesus is the only Son by nature. He is one of our kind. He is also one of a kind.

53

And lo a voice from heaven, saying, This is my beloved Son, in whom I am well pleased.

Matthew 3:17 (KJV)

And a voice from heaven said, "This is my Son, whom I love; with him I am well pleased."

Matthew 3:17 (NIV)

Jesus grew from a child to a boy and from a boy to a man. There is little known about his childhood. There is a lot known about his adulthood. Aged about thirty, Jesus of Nazareth comes to the River Jordan and offers himself for baptism by John the Baptist. John baptizes Jesus, and as he comes up from the water the heavens are opened. From heaven, the Father speaks words of affection over Jesus, telling him that he is his Son and that he is well pleased with him. This is an affirmation of existing sonship, not an adoption into new sonship. Jesus was already the one and only Son of the Father. From eternity to eternity Jesus alone is the Son by nature. What the Father is doing is revealing his unconditional acceptance of his Son as he embarks now on his three-year ministry. The Father's acceptance is based on the Son's position, not the Son's performance. God says, "I'm proud of you" even before Jesus has started his ministry!

54

*From that time Jesus began to preach, and to say,
Repent: for the kingdom of heaven is at hand.*

Matthew 4:17 (KJV)

**From that time on Jesus began to preach,
"Repent, for the kingdom of heaven is near."**

Matthew 4:17 (NIV)

After Jesus has been baptized he is tested by Satan for forty days and nights in the desert. Having successfully resisted, Jesus comes out of the wilderness and begins to preach the message of the kingdom of heaven. God already rules in heaven. He is on his royal throne and his reign is everlasting. But planet earth has been under Satan's rule since the temptation of Adam and Eve in the Garden. Now the reign of God is entering history. Heaven is invading earth through Jesus of Nazareth. The Son is bringing the Father's rule to planet earth and the Adversary's reign is now being directly confronted. Jesus tells his listeners that heaven's rule is very near to them and that they are to repent – they are to turn from self-rule (sin) to God's rule (the kingdom). In this kingdom, sins are forgiven, sicknesses are healed, poverty is eradicated, demons are expelled and even the dead are raised. The kingdom of God is truly heaven on earth.

55

Blessed are the meek: for they shall inherit the earth.

Matthew 5:5 (KJV)

Blessed are the meek, for they will inherit the earth.

Matthew 5:5 (NIV)

Jesus chooses twelve disciples or apprentices to follow him. These twelve men remind us of the twelve tribes of Israel. Jesus is accordingly fulfilling the calling that the Father gave to Israel. Here in Matthew chapters 5–7 Jesus teaches his famous Sermon on the Mount. This is a sermon in which he describes the kind of lifestyle expected of someone who enters the kingdom of heaven. Jesus tells the disciples that they will be blessed if they behave as the Father wants. "Blessed are the meek," he says. Meekness is not weakness. It is great strength harnessed to God's will. It is the word used for the reining in of a wild horse. "Blessed are those who allow themselves to be reined in by the LORD. They will inherit the earth." When Jesus returns at the end of history, those who have been harnessed to the work of the kingdom will live for ever and enjoy the full blessings of the new heavens and the new earth.

56

After this manner therefore pray ye: Our Father which art in heaven, Hallowed be thy name.

Matthew 6:9 (KJV)

This, then, is how you should pray: "Our Father in heaven, hallowed be your name..."

Matthew 6:9 (NIV)

The Lord's Prayer, beginning "Our Father", is the most famous prayer in history. Jesus is teaching his apprentices about prayer. They have seen him pray and they want to know how to do it too. Jesus tells them to begin by praying "Our Father". The word Jesus would have used is the Aramaic word *Abba*. Aramaic was the language Jesus spoke. *Abba* is an intimate word. It is the first word learned by a child in at least four Middle Eastern countries even to this day. It means "Daddy". Jesus taught his disciples to begin their prayers by addressing God in the most intimate, relational, and affectionate terms. He wanted them to hallow *Abba*'s name, to hold it sacred. And he wanted them to remember that God is a *heavenly* Father. Unlike earthly fathers, he is infinite, not finite, and he is perfect, not imperfect. All this shows that Jesus came to reveal that God is *Abba*, Father, and that God is relational, not remote.

57

But seek ye first the kingdom of God, and his righteousness; and all these things shall be added unto you.

Matthew 6:33 (KJV)

Seek first his kingdom and his righteousness, and all these things will be given to you as well.

Matthew 6:33 (NIV)

Jesus teaches his disciples that the greatest priority of their lives is to seek the kingdom of God. As children of the perfect Father, their first passion must always be to hunger and thirst for the reign and the righteousness of God on earth. This must begin in their lives first. The apprentices of Jesus must want to see the Father's rule coming into history and they must begin by placing everything that they are under God's rule. This means their character, their dreams, their relationships, their possessions, must be submitted to the loving reign of God. They must allow the Father's righteousness to become their own. When they do that, everything will be provided by their Father – clothes, food, and everything else besides. Those who follow Jesus must live counter-culturally. They must not seek material, temporary things (like money) first. That is what the world does. They must put first things first and pursue spiritual, eternal realities (like love) before all other things.

58

If ye then, being evil, know how to give good gifts unto your children, how much more shall your Father which is in heaven give good things to them that ask him?

Matthew 7:11 (KJV)

If you, then, though you are evil, know how to give good gifts to your children, how much more will your Father in heaven give good gifts to those who ask him!

Matthew 7:11 (NIV)

How is a person to obey the teachings of Jesus? Jesus tells his apprentices that they are to live a life that is more righteous than that of the Pharisees, the ultra-orthodox and observant Jews of his day. He says that the disciples must be authentic, living on the inside what they profess to be on the outside. How on earth does anyone achieve such a high calling? Jesus says that we have a Father who loves giving good gifts to his children. Even earthly fathers love doing that, and earthly fathers are imperfect. Unredeemed, earthly fathers are "evil" (or "sinful"). But our God is a perfect *Abba*, or Daddy, and if we ask him trustingly like a child he will give us the good gifts, the power of his Holy Spirit, with which to fulfil our calling. We will become more and more like the Son as we resolve to take on the characteristics of our Father with the help of the Holy Spirit.

59

Come unto me, all ye that labour and are heavy laden, and I will give you rest.

Matthew 11:28 (KJV)

Come to me, all you who are weary and burdened, and I will give you rest.

Matthew 11:28 (NIV)

This great invitation follows Jesus' words in Matthew 11:27: "All things have been committed to me by my Father. No-one knows the Son except the Father, and no-one knows the Father except the Son and those to whom the Son chooses to reveal him." Jesus has been celebrating the fact that his apprentices are hearing truths that have been hidden from the wise and the sophisticated. The Father has chosen to reveal his secrets to little children, to the disciples. Now Jesus teaches that no one can get to know *Abba* Father unless the Son introduces them to him. The Son reveals the Father. Once we have had a personal, direct revelation of the Father's love, all striving to earn God's approval comes to an end. The yoke becomes easy and the burden becomes light. Instead of resting from work, we work from rest. Revelation of the Father's love leads to a joyful spirituality of sabbath rest.

60

Verily I say unto you, Except ye be converted, and become as little children, ye shall not enter into the kingdom of heaven.

Matthew 18:3 (KJV)

I tell you the truth, unless you change and become like little children, you will never enter the kingdom of heaven.

Matthew 18:3 (NIV)

Jesus came not to start a religion but to start a relationship. He came to reveal *Abba* Father's love and to die on the Cross so that we could be reconciled to our Father in heaven. This is all about relationship. Jesus lived out of that deep, personal relationship with the Father. He wants us to as well. This is what Jesus is teaching his disciples here. He calls a little child to come and sit with him. The disciples are asking who is the greatest in the kingdom of heaven. Jesus' answer is to point at the child and tell the disciples that they cannot even enter the kingdom unless they become childlike. Their egos must decrease. Their pride must be crucified. The disciples must allow the Father to transform them so that they become one of his "little ones". Like Alice, in *Alice in Wonderland*, they will never enter into the enticing landscape of the kingdom unless they first become very small.

61

It is easier for a camel to go through the eye of a needle, than for a rich man to enter into the kingdom of God.

Mark 10:25 (KJV)

It is easier for a camel to go through the eye of a needle than for a rich man to enter the kingdom of God.

Mark 10:25 (NIV)

A rich man has just come to Jesus in the presence of the disciples. The man has asked Jesus what he must do to inherit eternal life. Jesus tells the man to sell all he has and give the money to the poor. The disciples are startled. How can a rich person enter the kingdom of God? Jesus then uses this striking word picture involving a camel passing through the eye of a needle. What did Jesus mean by that? A number of solutions have been offered: that it refers to a camel passing through a narrow mountain pass, or a small door fixed in a gate, or a sewing instrument. However, Jesus spoke in Aramaic, and the Aramaic word translated "camel" (*gamla*) can also be translated "rope". It may be that Jesus is saying that it is easier for a rope to go through the eye of a sewing needle than for a rich man to enter the kingdom of God. Whatever the right interpretation, Jesus not only came to comfort the afflicted; he came to afflict the comfortable.

62

And Jesus answering said unto them, Render to Caesar the things that are Caesar's, and to God the things that are God's.

Mark 12:17 (KJV)

Then Jesus said to them, "Give to Caesar what is Caesar's and to God what is God's."

Mark 12:17 (NIV)

In this episode, Jesus is being challenged by some opponents who are trying to catch him out. They ask him if they should pay taxes to Caesar. If he says yes, then he will be seen to be supporting the hated Roman occupiers. If he says no, then he will be seen to be committing treason. Jesus asks for a denarius, a coin. He asks whose image it bears. They reply, "Caesar's". He then utters the saying here about giving to Caesar and giving to God. Jesus seems to be saying it is right to pay taxes to the government of the day and it is also right to give to God. But there is more to it than this. There was an image of Caesar on the coin. The coin would therefore have been made "in the image of Caesar". Jesus knows that as human beings we are all made "in the image of God", who is far greater than Caesar. The money Caesar asks for is therefore nothing compared to what God asks for. God asks for everything from us because we are made in his image!

63

And he arose, and came to his father. But when he was yet a great way off, his father saw him, and had compassion, and ran, and fell on his neck, and kissed him.

Luke 15:20 (KJV)

So he got up and went to his father. But while he was still a long way off, his father saw him and was filled with compassion for him; he ran to his son, threw his arms around him and kissed him.

Luke 15:20 (NIV)

Jesus is being confronted by teachers of the law who are criticizing him for having meals with sinners. Jesus responds to his critics by telling three stories in Luke 15. The third one concerns a son who demands his inheritance from his father. In the Middle East, to ask this while your father is still alive is effectively to say, "I wish you were dead." The father, though, is magnificent. Day and night he waits for his boy to return. One day he sees his boy coming home, emaciated and ruined. He is filled with compassion and he lifts up his robe to run like the wind to greet him. He throws his arms around his wretched child's neck and kisses him repeatedly. What a picture! What a father! Jesus uses this story to tell his critics what God is really like. He is not the God that they have been portraying, who shuns the lost. He is the world's most amazing Father, like the father in Luke 15. He is the God of embrace, not exclusion.

64

Jesus answered and said unto him, Verily, verily, I say unto thee, Except a man be born again, he cannot see the kingdom of God.

John 3:3 (KJV)

In reply Jesus declared, "I tell you the truth, no-one can see the kingdom of God unless he is born again."

John 3:3 (NIV)

Jesus is visited by a member of the ruling council of the Pharisees called Nicodemus. Nicodemus comes to Jesus by night, no doubt because he does not want to be seen visiting this radical *hasid*, or holy man. Nicodemus acknowledges that Jesus of Nazareth is a man who has come from God because of the miracles that he has been performing. Jesus answers by telling Nicodemus that a person cannot see the kingdom of God unless they are born again. The kingdom of God and the Fatherhood of God are the two central themes of Jesus' teaching. God's kingdom refers to his reign on earth, evidenced by the miracles that Nicodemus has referenced. Jesus tells Nicodemus that he must be spiritually reborn if he is to witness the reality of the reign of heaven on earth. He must have a radical new start in which he puts his trust in Jesus and follows him. By the end of John's Gospel, Nicodemus will be bringing burial spices to venerate the dead Jesus.

65

For God so loved the world, that he gave his only begotten Son, that whosoever believeth in him should not perish, but have everlasting life.

John 3:16 (KJV)

For God so loved the world that he gave his one and only Son, that whoever believes in him shall not perish but have eternal life.

John 3:16 (NIV)

In this magnificent verse from the Gospel of John we are given an insight into the reason why God sent Jesus to the earth. First of all, we learn that God so *loved* the world. The Father couldn't stand to see humanity living in the orphan state any longer. This is because he loved the world – loved it in the sense of self-sacrificial love. So secondly he gave his one and only Son. The language here is reminiscent of the story of Abraham in Genesis 22. There Abraham was prepared to sacrifice his son Isaac out of obedience to God. Isaac is described as *yahid* in the Hebrew language, as Abraham's "one and only, precious one". Our Heavenly Father was prepared to give his precious one too. Thirdly, the Father gave what was dearest to him in order to save human beings from eternal separation from his love, from "perishing". What we need to do by way of response is to believe in Jesus and enter an eternal friendship with him.

66

*And Jesus said unto them, I am the bread of life:
he that cometh to me shall never hunger; and he
that believeth on me shall never thirst.*

John 6:35 (KJV)

**Then Jesus declared, "I am the bread of life. He
who comes to me will never go hungry, and he
who believes in me will never be thirsty."**

John 6:35 (NIV)

Jesus has performed a great miracle at the start of
John chapter 6: he has multiplied five loaves into
enough bread to feed 5,000 men (more like 15,000
people if you include the women and children as well).
This startles the crowd who follow Jesus across the
Lake of Galilee and catch up with him. They engage in
discussion with Jesus. Continuing the theme of bread,
they announce that Moses gave *manna* (supernatural
bread) to their forefathers in the wilderness after
their exodus from Egypt. Jesus tells them it wasn't
Moses who gave them this bread from heaven. It was
their heavenly Father. The crowd then say, "Give us
this bread." Jesus replies, "I am the Bread." Notice
the phrase, "I am". God revealed himself to Moses
as "I am who I am." Jesus is using the divine name
of himself here. He is telling his listeners that he is
divine. He is also telling them that he alone can satisfy
the spiritual hunger that they and all human beings
have.

67

The thief cometh not, but for to steal, and to kill, and to destroy: I am come that they might have life, and that they might have it more abundantly.

John 10:10 (KJV)

The thief comes only to steal and kill and destroy; I have come that they may have life, and have it to the full.

John 10:10 (NIV)

There are two words for "life" in the Greek language in which John's Gospel was originally written. There is first of all the word *bios*, from which we get the word "biology". This means finite, physical life. Then there is the word *zoe*, from which we get the word "zoology". This means infinite, spiritual life. In this famous saying Jesus announces that he has come to earth in order to give those who follow him a life that lasts for ever, an abundant life that satisfies the deepest longings of the human soul, a life that no worldly, material comforts can deliver. The devil does the exact opposite. He steals everything that gives a person life. He has come to the earth to steal, kill, and destroy. He has been doing that since the Garden of Eden, where he robbed our first parents of the life that the Father had given them. The good news is that Jesus is far stronger and has come to defeat the Adversary and to restore what the enemy has stolen.

68

Jesus wept.

John 11:35 (KJV)

Jesus wept.

John 11:35 (NIV)

This is the shortest verse in the Bible. It occurs in the context of the seventh miracle in John chapters 1–12 (seven is a number symbolic of perfection). Jesus has a close friend called Lazarus who lives in Bethany, just outside Jerusalem. While Jesus is far away, he receives a message that Lazarus is gravely ill. By the time he arrives, Lazarus has been dead four days and is lying in an enclosed tomb. Jesus raises him from the dead, but before he does so John records that he "wept". The original Greek verb *dakruo* is in fact stronger than that. It means "sobbed". The words "Jesus sobbed" tell us a great deal. Jesus is the one who reveals the Father. He shows us what God is really like. If Jesus weeps over Lazarus, then we know that God is not apathetic to our pain (like the God of the ancient Greeks) but sympathetic and even empathic. He feels what we feel. He is truly the Suffering God, "familiar with suffering" (Isaiah 53:3).

69

Jesus saith unto him, I am the way, the truth, and the life: no man cometh unto the Father, but by me.

John 14:6 (KJV)

Jesus answered, "I am the way and the truth and the life. No-one comes to the Father except through me."

John 14:6 (NIV)

There are seven "I am" sayings of Jesus in John's Gospel: "I am the Bread of Life," "I am the Light of the World," "I am the Good Shepherd," "I am the Gate," "I am the Resurrection and the Life," "I am the Way, the Truth and the Life," and "I am the True Vine." Jesus utters the sixth here. He has just been teaching his disciples that he is going to leave them. This is the night before he is crucified. He tells them that he is going ahead of them to prepare a place for them in his Father's house. He then tells them that he alone is the Way to the Father, the Truth about the Father, and the Life that the Father wants to bring to the world. No one can enter into a relationship with *Abba* Father except by coming to him. Notice Jesus does not say he is "*a* way", "*a* truth", "*a* life". He uses the definite article: "*the* Way, *the* Truth, *the* Life". Jesus is unashamed of his uniqueness in the context of the world's religions. He says he is "*the* way" to the Father, not just "*a* way"!

70

I will not leave you comfortless: I will come to you.

John 14:18 (KJV)

I will not leave you as orphans; I will come to you.

John 14:18 (NIV)

It is twenty-four hours before the crucifixion. Jesus meets with his disciples and washes their feet in an extraordinary act of humility and love (John 13). Then he begins to prepare his followers for his death and departure. In John 14 his note is one of reassurance. In verse 18 he promises his disciples that he will not leave them comfortless. The word literally means "as orphans". The word "orphan" in the Hebrew Bible means "without a father". Jesus is indicating here that all human beings are without a father. He is not referring to earthly fathers but to his Heavenly Father. Since the fall of Adam and Eve we have all lived in an orphan state spiritually. We have been separated from the true Father's love. However, Jesus is now about to die so that the barrier of sin can be removed and a way can be opened back to the Father. He promises they will no longer be orphans and that he will return to them.

71

*Peace I leave with you, my peace I give unto you:
not as the world giveth, give I unto you. Let not
your heart be troubled, neither let it be afraid.*

John 14:27 (KJV)

**Peace I leave with you; my peace I give you. I do
not give to you as the world gives. Do not let your
hearts be troubled and do not be afraid.**

John 14:27 (NIV)

Jesus continues speaking to his disciples in a part
of John's Gospel known as "the farewell discourses"
(chapters 13–17). These chapters are a record of Jesus'
final teachings to his apprentices within twenty-four
hours of his death on the Cross. He is seeking to bring
them comfort before the trauma of his execution.
Jesus tells his friends that he is giving them a special
kind of peace. The word "peace" here is a word that
was originally used to refer to the calm after a storm,
the resolving of discordant musical notes, and the
joining of hands in reconciliation after conflict. It is
a beautiful word harking back to the Hebrew word
shalom, which refers to peace at every level (with God,
neighbour, ourselves, and creation). Jesus says that
he alone can provide this kind of peace. Nothing the
world has to offer can give it. But he can. And this
remains true to this day.

72

Greater love hath no man than this, that a man lay down his life for his friends.

John 15:13 (KJV)

Greater love has no-one than this, that he lay down his life for his friends.

John 15:13 (NIV)

It was C. S. Lewis who wrote about the four great words in classical Greek that can be translated "love". There is *phileia*, which means the love of friends. There is *storge*, which means the nurturing affection of a mother. There is *eros*, which means the sexual love of passionate lovers. And there is *agape*, which refers to the self-forgetful love of the one who gives up everything in the service of others. It is this fourth word that is used here in this saying in John 15. Jesus tells his disciples that there is no greater love than the *agape* love shown by someone who sacrifices his life so that his friends might live. No wonder this saying is so often used at Remembrance Sunday services as people honour the sacrifice of those who have died in war so that others might be free. But the greatest demonstration of *agape* love was on the Cross, which Jesus is anticipating in these words.

73

For the Father himself loveth you, because ye have loved me, and have believed that I came out from God.

John 16:27 (KJV)

No, the Father himself loves you because you have loved me and have believed that I came from God.

John 16:27 (NIV)

Jesus now draws his farewell address to a close. He speaks openly about his return to the Father. In John's Gospel we are presented with a very clear journey: Jesus descends from the glorious realm of the Father and becomes a human being. He ministers for a number of years before returning to the Father at an hour appointed by the Father. This hour encompasses his death, resurrection, and ascension, which are all regarded as part of the lifting up of the Son of Man (i.e. Jesus). In John 16, Jesus is now very close to leaving and he tells his disciples that everything is about to change. In their relationship to him, they are no longer going to be servants but friends. In relation to God, the disciples are no longer going to be spiritual orphans; they are going to know that the Father loves them personally and dearly. This is all because they have chosen to love the Son and to believe that he has come from the Father.

74

And he said, Abba, Father, all things are possible
unto thee; take away this cup from me: nevertheless
not what I will, but what thou wilt.

Mark 14:36 (KJV)

"Abba, Father," he said, "everything is possible
for you. Take this cup from me. Yet not what I will,
but what you will."

Mark 14:36 (NIV)

We have seen that Jesus' premier word for God was
Abba, an Aramaic word meaning "Daddy". It was an
unusual word to use of God. Though there are hints of
the Father heart of God in the Old Testament, no one
before Jesus had dared to be so familiar, intimate, and
affectionate in addressing Almighty God. Here in Mark
14 we see Jesus in the Garden of Gethsemane on the
night of his arrest and trial. He knows what lies ahead.
The task the Father has given him is almost complete.
His mission to rescue the world from sin is almost
done. But just as he prepares for the final twenty-
four hours he finds himself in agony of soul as he
contemplates the horrors of his impending suffering.
He comes to God as *Abba*, as "Daddy". He wrestles
with his mission with a troubled heart, asking for the
cup of suffering to pass. He then submits himself to
the Father's will: "Not my will but yours be done." The
Son is truly obedient to his Father from beginning to
end.

75

And at the ninth hour Jesus cried with a loud voice, saying, Eloi, Eloi, lama sabachthani? which is, being interpreted, My God, my God, why hast thou forsaken me?

Mark 15:34 (KJV)

At the ninth hour Jesus cried out in a loud voice, "Eloi, Eloi, lama sabachthani?" – which means, "My God, my God, why have you forsaken me?"

Mark 15:34 (NIV)

After Jesus has prayed he is arrested in the Garden of Gethsemane. He endures an early morning Roman trial in which he is condemned to death and flogged. Jesus is nailed to a wooden cross on a hill known as the Place of the Skull outside Jerusalem. The suffering he went through must have been unimaginably extreme. Much of this would have been physical, and no doubt emotional too. But here we see the spiritual agony of Jesus as he hangs on the Cross. He cries out using words from Psalm 22 verse 1, "My God, My God, why have you abandoned me?" As Jesus takes the sin of the world on his shoulders, he becomes aware in his humanity that he no longer senses the Father's intimate presence. At this moment, he embraces all the abandonment of the orphan, human condition. He who was the Son by nature experiences abandonment so that we who are spiritual orphans might find our heart's true home in the Father's love.

76

And Jesus said unto him, Verily I say unto thee, To day shalt thou be with me in paradise.

Luke 23:43 (KJV)

Jesus answered him, "I tell you the truth, today you will be with me in paradise."

Luke 23:43 (NIV)

There are seven final statements spoken by Jesus on the Cross: "Father, forgive them," "You will be with me in paradise," "Woman, behold your son," "My God, my God, why have you forsaken me?" "I thirst," "It is finished," and "Father, into your hands I commit my spirit." Here we see the crucified Jesus flanked by two condemned thieves. One of them is hard-hearted and tells Jesus to save himself and them. The other is appalled at these words and turns to Jesus, saying, "Remember me when you come into your kingdom." Jesus replies with this memorable saying: "Today you will be with me in paradise." Paradise was regarded as an Eden-like garden of perfect peace, prosperity, and repose. Jesus tells the penitent criminal that not only will they be together in death; they will also be together in life. And there will be no waiting, nor any intermediate state of preparation. Today they are on a bleak hill dying. In the twinkling of an eye they are going to be in a beautiful garden, alive for evermore.

77

Jesus saith unto her, Touch me not; for I am not yet ascended to my Father: but go to my brethren and say unto them, I ascend unto my Father, and your Father; and to my God, and your God.

John 20:17 (KJV)

Jesus said, "Do not hold on to me, for I have not yet returned to the Father. Go instead to my brothers and tell them, 'I am returning to my Father and your Father, to my God and your God.'"

John 20:17 (NIV)

This statement comes at the close of one of the most poignant scenes in the Gospels. Jesus has died and his body has been buried in a garden tomb. Two days later, in the early hours of the first Easter Sunday morning, Mary Magdalene (a female follower) goes to the tomb to weep there. She meets someone who she thinks is the gardener, but it turns out to be Jesus. He has been raised from the dead and calls her by name. At the mention of her name, Mary is overcome with joy and tries to embrace Jesus. Jesus tells her to stop holding him, because everything has now changed in her relationship with him and indeed with God. Her communion will now be with the Father that Jesus has been talking about throughout his ministry. Mary, and all who follow Jesus, will now be able to relate to God as Jesus did, in an intimate, spiritual communion with *Abba* Father. With the resurrection of Jesus, it's as if the world has begun again.

MAP OF ISRAEL IN THE TIME
OF THE NEW TESTAMENT

78

And, being assembled together with them, [he] commanded them that they should not depart from Jerusalem, but wait for the promise of the Father, which, saith he, ye have heard of me.

Acts 1:4 (KJV)

On one occasion, while he was eating with them, he gave them this command: "Do not leave Jerusalem, but wait for the gift my Father promised, which you have heard me speak about."

Acts 1:4 (NIV)

Momentous days followed hard after the first Easter, when Jesus was raised from the dead. On many occasions his disciples saw him alive, in his resurrection body. Over a period of forty days, Luke the historian (the author of the Book of Acts) tells us that Jesus gave his followers many convincing proofs that he was alive. Acts 1 verse 4 describes one of these confirming encounters. Luke tells us that the risen Jesus came and met with his disciples to instruct them concerning what was about to happen. He even ate with them. As he did so, he told them to wait in Jerusalem, even though it was the city associated with so much suffering. They were to wait until the Father's promised gift arrived – the gift of the Holy Spirit. Ten days later, after Jesus had ascended to heaven in front of their very eyes, the Holy Spirit fell upon the earliest followers of Jesus and they were filled with the fire of love.

79

*But ye shall receive power, after that the Holy
Ghost is come upon you: and ye shall be witnesses
unto me both in Jerusalem, and in all Judaea, and
in Samaria, and unto the uttermost part of the
earth.*

Acts 1:8 (KJV)

**But you will receive power when the Holy Spirit
comes on you; and you will be my witnesses in
Jerusalem, and in all Judea and Samaria, and to
the ends of the earth.**

Acts 1:8 (NIV)

Shortly before Jesus returns to his Father in heaven,
he tells his disciples that a day is coming when they
are going to be baptized in the Holy Spirit. The word
"baptize" means to "drench". The "Holy Spirit" refers
to the empowering, personal presence of God. Jesus
is accordingly forewarning his apprentices that they
are about to receive an overwhelming experience
of the Father's love and power in their lives. This
experience will be totally immersive and it will inspire
them to be brave witnesses to the resurrection of
Jesus. This is what the earliest Christians received,
and indeed what every Christian since is to receive –
an empowerment of the Holy Spirit which enables us
to communicate the good news about Jesus locally,
regionally, nationally, and globally. This is the task of
the church. The church is not a social club full of nice
people who do good works. It is a courageous band of
heralds proclaiming the Lordship of Jesus in Spirit-
empowered words.

80

This Jesus hath God raised up, whereof we all are witnesses.

Acts 2:32 (KJV)

God has raised this Jesus to life, and we are all witnesses of the fact.

Acts 2:32 (NIV)

After the Holy Spirit falls upon the 120 disciples in Jerusalem, Simon Peter stands up to speak. He begins to give his first sermon to a huge crowd in the city of Jerusalem. He is bold in speaking about the fire that has just fallen, telling his listeners that all this is in fulfilment of what the prophet Joel predicted about God pouring out his Spirit on all flesh. He is then equally bold in preaching about Jesus – the Jesus who ministered in Israel, who died on the Cross, who rose from the dead, who ascended into heaven, and who is both messiah and Lord. Peter tells his listeners that Jesus is risen and alive and that he and others are all witnesses to that fact. No counter-argument is brought forward, because there is none. Peter's boldness wins the crowd over. The Peter who denied Jesus a matter of weeks before is now boldly proclaiming him. Only something life-changing could have done that to Peter.

81

While Peter yet spake these words, the Holy Ghost fell on all them which heard the word.

Acts 10:44 (KJV)

While Peter was still speaking these words, the Holy Spirit came on all who heard the message.

Acts 10:44 (NIV)

The earliest Christians now start carrying the message of the Good News to the world. In doing this they experience a watershed in Acts 10. Here Simon Peter has a vision in which the Father tells him that he is not to call those who are non-Jewish "unclean". The Father loves everyone and Peter is to break down dividing racial walls and take God's love to the Gentiles. So Peter goes to the household of a Roman centurion called Cornelius and preaches there. While he is speaking the Holy Spirit comes upon the Gentile listeners just as had happened with the Jewish followers of Jesus at Pentecost (Acts 2). The author says that the Holy Spirit 'fell upon' the Gentiles (see KJV above). This is the same verb which is used in Luke 15:20 of the father falling upon the neck of the returning, prodigal son. Here the Holy Spirit brings the affection of *Abba* Father to the Gentiles for the first time.

82

For I am not ashamed of the gospel of Christ: for it is the power of God unto salvation to every one that believeth; to the Jew first, and also to the Greek.

Romans 1:16 (KJV)

I am not ashamed of the gospel, because it is the power of God for the salvation of everyone who believes: first for the Jew, then for the Gentile.

Romans 1:16 (NIV)

The greatest event in the New Testament outside the Gospels is without doubt the conversion of Saul of Tarsus. Saul had been persecuting the church but had an encounter with the risen Jesus on the road to Damascus. This changed his life and his name. He became Paul the Apostle. Here Paul tells us that he is fearlessly unashamed of proclaiming the gospel of Christ. In the ancient world, "gospel" was a word used for the announcement of a Roman military victory somewhere in the empire – a victory that established *Pax Romana*, the Roman rule of peace. In the New Testament it is used to describe the Christian's declaration that Christ has vanquished the evil powers of this universe and has established God's rule of peace. Paul's gospel is the gospel not of Caesar but of Christ. When it is heard and believed, it has the power to transform human lives completely. And this gospel is inclusive: it is for everyone, Jew and Gentile.

83

For ye have not received the spirit of bondage again to fear; but ye have received the Spirit of adoption, whereby we cry, Abba, Father.

Romans 8:15 (KJV)

For you did not receive a spirit that makes you a slave again to fear, but you received the Spirit of sonship. And by him we cry, "Abba, Father."

Romans 8:15 (NIV)

Paul is writing to the Romans about their relationship with *Abba*, Father. He has just been telling them that they should not live according to the inclinations of their sinful flesh. They should live lives directed by the Holy Spirit. He makes the point that those who are led by the Spirit of God are the sons of God. In other words, those who are truly in relationship with *Abba*, Father allow the Holy Spirit to direct their choices and their conduct. He then proceeds to tell them that they really are sons (and of course daughters) of God. They have been rescued and redeemed from slavery and they have been adopted by *Abba*, Father through the work of Jesus Christ. They now have the Spirit at work within their hearts (Romans 5:5), and this Spirit is the one whom John Wesley called "the loving Spirit of Adoption". This Spirit ignites our hearts with the flame of love and enables us to call God *Abba*, or Daddy.

84

*The Spirit itself beareth witness with our spirit,
that we are the children of God.*

Romans 8:16 (KJV)

**The Spirit himself testifies with our spirit that we
are God's children.**

Romans 8:16 (NIV)

Here Paul speaks about the role of the Holy Spirit in
our adoption. Paul has in mind the Roman practice
of adoption in which a couple would approach one
of their slaves and ask to adopt their son. The slave
would invariably say yes, because his child would be
rescued from the dangerous state of slavery. When the
exchange happened it followed a process in which the
natural father sold his boy three times to the adopting
father. All this would be done in the presence of seven
witnesses before being signed by a magistrate. The
magistrate would ask these witnesses if the adoption
process had been formally completed. They would
confirm this, and the slave's child would become the
son of a freeman. Here Paul tells us that the Holy
Spirit is the witness of our adoption. He testifies in
our spirits that we are the adopted children of God.
He is the love of the Father poured out in our hearts
(Romans 5:5).

85

For the earnest expectation of the creature waiteth for the manifestation of the sons of God.

Romans 8:19 (KJV)

The creation waits in eager expectation for the sons of God to be revealed.

Romans 8:19 (NIV)

In the time-frame between the first coming of Jesus and his second coming (on the last day of history), Paul teaches that the whole of creation is groaning like a woman in labour pains. There is a longing throughout the earth for the Son to return and for this fallen universe to be recreated as the new heavens and the new earth. As creation waits, it does so with "eager expectation". The word here is used of someone straining on tiptoe to see something ahead on the distant horizon. Paul of course is speaking here figuratively, not literally. He doesn't regard creation as a literal, living soul. But he does regard creation as frustrated in its fallen state, forever falling into decay, and he sees it as expectant for that day when *Abba* Father's adopted sons and daughters will be revealed. When that happens, the world will enter into the fulfilment of all its longings. Then the planet will hear Jesus say, "Behold, I make all things new!"

THE 100 VERSE BIBLE

86

*For I am persuaded, that neither death, nor life,
nor angels, nor principalities, nor powers, nor things
present, nor things to come, nor height, nor depth, nor
any other creature, shall be able to separate us from
the love of God, which is in Christ Jesus our Lord.*

Romans 8:38–39 (KJV)

**For I am convinced that neither death nor life,
neither angels nor demons, neither the present
nor the future, nor any powers, neither height nor
depth, nor anything else in all creation, will be
able to separate us from the love of God that is in
Christ Jesus our Lord.**

Romans 8:38–39 (NIV)

Romans chapter 8 is one of the greatest chapters of
the Bible. It begins with Paul announcing that there
is no condemnation for those who are in Christ
Jesus. It ends with him declaring that there is no
separation. What kind of separation is he referring to?
He is talking about separation from the Father's love.
This separation between the Father and all human
beings has come to an end in the glorious death
and resurrection of Jesus Christ. The first Adam's
sin had caused this separation, but now a Second
Adam – Jesus Christ – has come and paid the penalty
for sin on the Cross. Now there is nothing that can
ever separate a true believer from the Father's love
revealed in Jesus Christ. Paul is utterly convinced that
this is true. The millennia of separation have ended. A
new age has dawned. A new creation has occurred,
and now those who are "in Christ" will never again be
separated from the Father's love.

87

Though I speak with the tongues of men and of angels, and have not charity, I am become as sounding brass, or a tinkling cymbal.

1 Corinthians 13:1 (KJV)

If I speak in the tongues of men and of angels, but have not love, I am only a resounding gong or a clanging cymbal.

1 Corinthians 13:1 (NIV)

1 Corinthians 13 is one of the best-known chapters in the Bible. It is a fine passage in praise of true love and for that reason is often read at weddings. Here Paul is writing to the church in Corinth and he is teaching them about how to use the gifts of the Spirit wisely – supernatural gifts such as speaking in tongues, prophesying, and performing miracles. More than excelling in such gifts, Paul urges his readers to excel in love for one another. The King James Version renders the Greek word *agape as* "charity". Today we would call it "self-sacrificial love". This is the Christian's characteristic and unique word for love. Here in verse 1 Paul says that no language, either earthly or heavenly, can compare with the practice of Christ-like love. "If I speak eloquently or speak in tongues, and I do not excel in self-giving love, then I'm nothing but an echoing gong or clanging metal."

88

And [I] will be a Father unto you, and ye shall be my sons and daughters, saith the Lord Almighty.

2 Corinthians 6:18 (KJV)

I will be a Father to you, and you will be my sons and daughters, says the Lord Almighty.

2 Corinthians 6:18 (NIV)

2 Corinthians is a letter in which Paul really wears his heart on his sleeve. Here he implores his readers not to have anything to do with people who lead them astray but to separate themselves from them. At the end of the chapter he strings together three quotations from the Old Testament with the intention of showing that God longs for intimate communion with them, but that this intimacy is dependent upon their purity. In the last of the three, Paul quotes a prophecy given to King David in 2 Samuel 7:14: "I will be a father to him and he will be my son." Paul makes his readers the recipients of this prophecy and says, "You will be my sons." Paul also adds "and my daughters". God longs to be a Father to both men and women. He wants an affectionate relationship with both daughters and sons. Perhaps no verse sums up the love story of the entire Bible better than this.

89

Having predestinated us unto the adoption of children by Jesus Christ to himself, according to the good pleasure of his will...

Ephesians 1:5 (KJV)

He predestined us to be adopted as his sons through Jesus Christ, in accordance with his pleasure and will.

Ephesians 1:5 (NIV)

The letter to the Ephesians begins with a magnificent prayer of thanksgiving. The author begins, "Blessed be the God and Father of our Lord Jesus Christ." He then goes on to thank the Father for all the blessings we have "in Christ". The first thing he mentions is in verses 4 and 5. He praises God for choosing a people to be his own before the world was even made. He talks about how the Father predestined us for adoption. The author was once again thinking of the Roman practice of adoption here – a process in which the son of a slave was bought out of servitude and placed in a new family, with a new father. All previous debts were cancelled and the adopted son became the heir to his new parents' fortune. The author uses this as a picture to describe how followers of Jesus have been given a brand new Father and a brand new family. This plan of adoption gave *Abba*, Father great pleasure and joy.

90

For we are his workmanship, created in Christ Jesus unto good works, which God hath before ordained that we should walk in them.

Ephesians 2:10 (KJV)

For we are God's workmanship, created in Christ Jesus to do good works, which God prepared in advance for us to do.

Ephesians 2:10 (NIV)

This verse comes at the end of a passage in which Paul tells us how we have been saved by grace. Grace is the undeserved love of Jesus. Good works did not secure our salvation. What Jesus did at the Cross has achieved that. What we have to do for our part is put our faith in Christ's amazing grace. We are called to believe that Jesus has paid the price for our sins. Then we will be saved from a life of gratifying the desires of our sinful nature. And we will not only be rescued *from* something. We will be rescued *to* something as well – a life of doing the good works which the Father has prepared in advance for us to do. We are accordingly not saved *by* good works but we are saved *to* good works. And when we are saved, we become God's workmanship. The word in Greek is *poema*, from which we get our word "poem". As redeemed sons and daughters, we are the Father's masterpieces!

91

Put on the whole armour of God, that ye may be able to stand against the wiles of the devil.

Ephesians 6:11 (KJV)

Put on the full armour of God so that you can take your stand against the devil's schemes.

Ephesians 6:11 (NIV)

Paul knows that as Christians we are engaged in a ferocious spiritual war between light and darkness. On the Cross, Jesus Christ has conquered the dark forces of this universe. Though Satan has been defeated through the death and resurrection of Jesus, he still fights on and will continue to do so until the last day of history, when he is finally destroyed. In the meantime, Christians have to fight the good fight. We are not left ill-equipped or alone in this war. We are given the mighty power of the Holy Spirit. We are also given items of spiritual armour. Thinking of the Roman soldiers of his own day, Paul lists the items of our spiritual armour: a breastplate (righteousness), a belt (truth), shoes (peace), a helmet (salvation), a shield (faith), and a sword (God's word). With these resources we become part of the Father's army, eradicating evil not with the love of power but with the power of love.

92

Now faith is the substance of things hoped for, the evidence of things not seen.

Hebrews 11:1 (KJV)

Now faith is being sure of what we hope for and certain of what we do not see.

Hebrews 11:1 (NIV)

In this saying from the letter to the Hebrews, the author summarizes what faith is. Faith is the act of believing that what you cannot yet see is real. Christians believe that Jesus Christ is real. They believe that he is risen from the dead and alive for evermore. They cannot yet see him physically. But one day they will. The act of believing requires that we put our trust in something (or, better still, someone) invisible. The reward of believing is that we eventually see the one that we have believed in. The Bible teaches that Jesus Christ will return at the end of history on the clouds and in great glory. On that day, all those who have been sure of what they hoped for will see him. All those who have been certain of what they haven't seen will see him. So while sceptics say, "I'll believe it when I see it," the Christian says, "I'll see it when I believe it."

93

Pure religion and undefiled before God and the Father is this, To visit the fatherless and widows in their affliction, and to keep himself unspotted from the world.

James 1:27 (KJV)

Religion that God our Father accepts as pure and faultless is this: to look after orphans and widows in their distress and to keep oneself from being polluted by the world.

James 1:27 (NIV)

The letter of James stresses that a person whose faith is "alive" will do good works for the Father. James nowhere says that we are saved from our sins by good works. But he does teach us that we are saved *unto* good works. In other words, once a person is saved and adopted into the Father's family, they will inevitably seek to do the Father's will. One of the clearest descriptions of the kind of good works that James has in mind is in this verse. Here we learn what kind of religion the Father accepts as real: when believers care for the two groups of people for whom the Father has a special affection, orphans and widows. Until the return of Jesus Christ, Christians are to busy themselves with showing compassion in practical ways to the wounded and the broken-hearted. To do that, Christians must keep themselves from being defiled by the selfish values of a fallen world.

94

For the Lord himself shall descend from heaven with a shout, with the voice of the archangel, and with the trump of God: and the dead in Christ shall rise first.

1 Thessalonians 4:16 (KJV)

For the Lord himself will come down from heaven, with a loud command, with the voice of the archangel and with the trumpet call of God, and the dead in Christ will rise first.

1 Thessalonians 4:16 (NIV)

According to the New Testament, history is marching towards a momentous climax. It will begin with the return of Jesus on the last day. When this happens, there will be a noise enough to wake the dead – literally. There will be a loud command, the voice of the archangel, and the trumpet call of God! The loud command is like the shout of an officer to his troops. In this context it refers to Jesus issuing the order for the dead to rise. This command will be accompanied by the Archangel (most likely Michael) sounding God's trumpet. In the Old Testament, when God came down to meet his people it was sometimes accompanied by a trumpet blast (Exodus 19:16). Imagine a deafening, reverberating sound throughout the universe as Jesus comes back. The Lord's return will accordingly be audible as well as visible. Those who have died in Christ will rise to meet Jesus first. They will be followed by those who are still alive and who know the Lord.

95

Let no man deceive you by any means: for that day shall not come, except there come a falling away first, and that man of sin be revealed, the son of perdition.

2 Thessalonians 2:3 (KJV)

Don't let anyone deceive you in any way, for that day will not come until the rebellion occurs and the man of lawlessness is revealed, the man doomed to destruction.

2 Thessalonians 2:3 (NIV)

Before Jesus returns, there will be a period of extreme turmoil on the earth known as the Great Tribulation. This will involve a worldwide rebellion. This rebellion will be the final attempt of the enemy to tempt human beings into sinful independence from the Father. Paul says the "day" (namely the day of the Son's return) will not happen until a global falling away of uncommitted believers has occurred. He adds that a "man of lawlessness" will appear in that time, a man "doomed to destruction". Lawlessness is in effect rebellion against all authority. Satan will inspire this man of lawlessness to be utterly opposed to the Father and the Son. He will be a shameless blasphemer against God. He will be the Anti-Christ. He will have a period of dominance on the world scene, but at the return of Jesus he will be completely defeated and destroyed.

96

Love not the world, neither the things that are in the world. If any man love the world, the love of the Father is not in him.

1 John 2:15 (KJV)

Do not love the world or anything in the world. If anyone loves the world, the love of the Father is not in him.

1 John 2:15 (NIV)

Here John sets up a contrast. Christians daily have to choose between loving the world and loving the Father. What the world has to offer is nothing in comparison with what *Abba* Father has to offer. The world traps us in the enticing but deadly grip of addiction, specifically addiction to the idols of power, sex, and money. But the Father draws us with cords of love into a relationship in which we are seized by the power of the greatest affection of all – the love of the Father. While the world fills the hole in the soul with the worship of idols, Christians ask the Father to fill up their hearts with liquid waves of love. Those who are the children of God are accordingly to live in a state of detachment from this world, and in a state of attachment to the love that the world is looking for in all the wrong places.

97

Behold, what manner of love the Father hath bestowed upon us, that we should be called the sons of God: therefore the world knoweth us not, because it knew him not.

1 John 3:1 (KJV)

How great is the love the Father has lavished on us, that we should be called children of God! And that is what we are! The reason the world does not know us is that it did not know him.

1 John 3:1 (NIV)

John captures our attention with the little word, "look", or "behold". He goes on to ask, "What kind of love is this?" He is referring to the Father's love – a love that created the world and a love that has now redeemed the world in Christ. John becomes eloquent and lyrical about this love. He says that the Father has bestowed upon us the love of all loves. Actually, the word "bestowed" is a little weak. The verb does not just mean "granted". It means "lavished", as the New International Version renders it. The Father has poured his affections out upon us, and the proof is that those who have accepted his Son have now become the children of God. They have become sons and daughters by adoption. The world does not recognize these sons and daughters, but then the world didn't recognize the Son, Jesus, either. How wonderful it is to be loved by the world's greatest Father!

98

There is no fear in love; but perfect love casteth out fear: because fear hath torment. He that feareth is not made perfect in love.

1 John 4:18 (KJV)

There is no fear in love. But perfect love drives out fear, because fear has to do with punishment. The one who fears is not made perfect in love.

1 John 4:18 (NIV)

One of the great themes of the first letter of John is assurance – especially assurance of our salvation from sin and of our status as sons and daughters of the High King of Heaven. Here John sets up a striking contrast between two states of mind – being afraid and being loved. He says that Christians are not to be afraid. Of what, in particular? Of being punished. Christians are not to live in fear that God will condemn them. Jesus has taken their punishment at Calvary. Any judgment that was coming to them has been absorbed by the crucified body of Jesus. Instead, Christians are to know that they are dearly loved – eternally loved by *Abba* Father, who will never condemn them. This love expels fear. As the end of history draws nearer, Christians are more and more called to live in the assurance of the Father's love, not in toxic fear. This love perfects them: it makes them whole, complete, and at peace.

99

And I saw the dead, small and great, stand before God; and the books were opened: and another book was opened, which is the book of life: and the dead were judged out of those things which were written in the books, according to their works.

Revelation 20:12 (KJV)

And I saw the dead, great and small, standing before the throne, and books were opened. Another book was opened, which is the book of life. The dead were judged according to what they had done as recorded in the books.

Revelation 20:12 (NIV)

The Bible teaches that there are four final facts that await the world at the end of time: the return of Jesus Christ, the resurrection of the dead, the last judgment, and the creation of the new heavens and earth. In Revelation 20, Satan has just been thrown into the lake of fire. He is now finally, completely defeated and destroyed. The orphan-maker can do no more harm and reap no more havoc on planet earth. Now, before the great white throne, the last judgment begins. All are judged, both the great (in the world's eyes) and the small. God has two books: a record of all our deeds, and the book of life. This is a reminder that we write our own destinies in this life. We must choose today to step out of our orphan state and live as sons and daughters of God. The Father knows his children. Their names are engraved upon his hand and written in his book for ever.

100

And God shall wipe away all tears from their eyes; and there shall be no more death, neither sorrow, nor crying, neither shall there be any more pain: for the former things are passed away

Revelation 21:4 (KJV)

He will wipe every tear from their eyes. There will be no more death or mourning or crying or pain, for the old order of things has passed away.

Revelation 21:4 (NIV)

And when all is said and done, and the new heavens and the new earth have been created out of our own heaven and earth, there will be a final great display of the Father's love. From heaven the Father, the Son and the Holy Spirit will come to this renewed creation and make their home with us. A city will descend from heaven and be rooted here – a city where there will be no more suffering, no more crying, no more pain and no more dying. Here, in a city without a cemetery, the Father will come to us and look into our eyes with indescribable compassion. He will wipe away all our tears. Our orphan hearts will be healed. And in his gaze, a thousand painful memories will disappear like the mist of a new dawn. It will be the happiest and most glorious of days. And it will not be the end of the adventure. It will be just the beginning.

CONCLUSION:
A LETTER FROM OUR FATHER
(Based on the 100 verses)

My Beloved Child,
Even before the foundations of the world I was thinking
    of you.
I created the heavens and the earth as your home and I
    made you in my own image;
I created your frame and breathed life into your soul.
All this I did out of love so that I could be your Father
    and you could be my child.
Even though my children chose to depart from me, I
    have never forgotten them and I have never
    forgotten you;
My plan has always been to rescue my wayward sons
    and daughters,
Because my love is a promise-keeping, covenant love.
I promised Abraham that through him I would bless
    every nation under the sun,
And when Israel was in Egypt, oppressed by Pharaoh, I
    raised up Moses to deliver my people,
For my people are my adopted children, my very own.
I led them towards a land flowing with milk and honey
Like a father carrying a child upon his shoulders.
I made them a kingdom of priests and a holy nation.
I promised I would bless them if they kept my laws,
For I am compassionate and gracious,
Slow to anger,
Abounding in love and faithfulness,
And I am jealous for those whom I call my children.
I smile upon those who obey me.
I said to my people of old what I say to you today,
Be strong and very courageous,

For I am with you;
I am your Father.
My goodness and mercy follow you all the days of your
     life
And you will one day live in my house forever.
When others forsake you, I will not;
When earthly fathers and mothers abandon you, I will
     hold you close,
For I am the Father to the fatherless,
The defender of the cause of widows,
And the one who has compassion on his children.
For I knew you before you were born,
I formed you in your mother's womb,
All your days were written down in my Book of Life
     before you took your first breath,
And I long to give you the desires of your heart.
So trust in me;
Even a mighty flood could never drown the love that I
     have for you.
I am always ready to hear, to forgive and to heal.
Even when you feel all alone, I am there;
I am your everlasting Father,
And you are the work of my hands.
I rejoice over you with singing,
And I quiet you with my love.
For I know the plans that I have for you and my plans
     are good,
They are to prosper you, not to harm you.
All I ask is that you let me write my law upon your
     hearts
Because I want to put a new spirit within you,
And turn your heart of stone to a heart of flesh.
I want to reveal my secrets to you
And to give you my Holy Spirit as your helper.
Do not grieve, for my joy is your strength.

I sent my Son Jesus into the world to give you my peace;
He is the Lord of the heavens and the earth,
Yet he was born as a baby.
He came and dwelt among you.
I declared him to be my beloved Son, the pride of my life
And appointed him to usher in my reign on the earth.
He is the one who truly transforms the human soul;
Listen to him.
Learn to speak to me as your dearest Father,
And seek as my children to bring heaven to earth.
Ask me for what you need in this task
And do all that you do from a place of rest and security
    in my love.
Live as little children before me.
Do not pursue worldly idols
But put me first in your life.
I want to show you my compassion and affection
As only a perfect Father can.
I loved you so much that I sent my one and only Son
That you might live forever with me.
Everything you need you can only find in my Son,
For he came to bring you life – abundant life.
He alone reveals my Father heart;
He alone is the Way to my love.
I sent him so that you would no longer be a spiritual
    orphan
And so that your heart would not be troubled again.
He laid down his life for you
So that you would know that I love you dearly.
He drank the cup of deepest sorrow,
Embraced the pain of absolute desolation,
So that all your sins might be forgiven
And so that you and I could enjoy Paradise together.
Because of what my Son did on the Cross
You can know me as he knows me,

As your Father.
I sent my Holy Spirit just as I promised
So that your heart would be captured by my love
And your mouth would speak of my Son.
Be bold as a witness of my love;
Do not be ashamed of the Good News of my Son,
For I have delivered you from fear
And adopted you out of my great love
So that you might call me Abba, Daddy,
So that you would be sure that you are mine,
And I am yours.
So take my love to this broken world;
The whole of creation is waiting for you.
Nothing that opposes you will ever separate you from
*   my love,*
For my love is patient and kind,
My love is self-giving and eternal.
Ever since the world began
My plan has been to say to you
"I am your Father".
I predestined you for your adoption
And the thought of that made me smile with joy.
You are my poetry;
You are my song;
You are my masterpiece;
You are my work of art.
I have prepared an assignment for you;
Put on my armour and fight for the cause of my love.
Stand firm against the Adversary,
For his days are numbered.
Believe in me even though you cannot yet see me
And take my love to the orphan and the widow.
All this I call you to do until the final day
When out of heaven my Son will come
And the dead will be raised.
Though there may be great trouble before that day,

Hold fast to your love for me,
For I have lavished my love on you
And I will always lavish my love on you.
When the storm clouds begin to gather in the world,
Rest in my perfect love
And do not be afraid;
For my Son is coming soon
And he will judge the earth.
The enemy will be no more,
There will be no more tears,
And you and I will be face to face in the end,
Just as it was in the beginning.

I am your Father,
You are my child,
I love you,
And I will never stop loving you.

With endless love,
From
Abba, Father